Major Contributors to Social Science Series

ALFRED MC CLUNG LEE, General Editor

Preface

Acknowledged as the "father" of sociology as a scientific subject matter, Auguste Comte is nevertheless probably less well known in any detail today among students of sociology than other leading sociological thinkers of the nineteenth and twentieth centuries. The single-volume American textbooks on sociological theory or on the history of sociology generally make short shrift of him, contenting themselves mainly with reiterating his law of the three stages (or states) and his classification of the sciences, with a bow or two in the direction of his concepts of social statics and dynamics as the bases for a scientific sociology. Some of them, in announcing that he was a "positivist," have then incorrectly spelled out the meaning he gave to the epithet. Others have fallen into sad error by making him out to be the father of modern neo-positivism, especially in sociology, and even of mathematical sociology, something he looked on with jaundiced eye as a misinterpretation of sociology's concern with the internal dynamics of human nature and with man's resulting relationship with other men.

To know Comte's writings is indispensable to an understanding today of both sociology in general and of research and explanation in its subsidiary fields since the path upon which Comte set sociology is just now being recognized as its most significant. This path leads us through an understanding of sociology as scientific knowledge for social control, through the need for a general theoretical framework from which to derive working hypotheses for social research, through sociology's inextricable connections with other sciences—particularly biology and psychology, and finally to sociology's full-blooded connection with history and to its use in the foundation of ancillary sciences such as economics, politics, anthropology, and even archaeology.

The contemporary neglect of Comte, by American sociologists in particular, has led to his being taken over by intellectual historians who are all too often interested in ideological curiosities rather than in science. This can be seen even in such a learned book as W. M. Simon's *European Positivism in the Nineteenth Century, An Essay in Intellectual History*. But Simon is far superior in his appreciation of Comte to some other intellectual historians when he concludes:

Hunger for systematic and comprehensive explanation was the distinctive hallmark of the Positivist. Likewise, it was his insistence on providing and on imposing such an explanation that was the distinctive hallmark of Comte himself, setting him apart from the exponents of mere scientism. It was this insistence that determined everything he wrote, and equally everything he did. It determined the vicissitudes of his teaching after his death and the violence with which people tended to disagree about it. It made sure that anyone who considered Positivism seriously at all was bound to confront ultimate questions not only of the intellect but also of temperament, and that even those who rejected it outright were bound to hold to their divergent opinions with a more enlightened awareness of their nature and implications. And it is perhaps ultimately the function of attempts at comprehensive explanation to allow people, not to swallow them whole, but to sharpen their teeth on them. In this sense it is not altogether idle to award marks for effort rather than for success, and of the heroism of Comte's effort there can be no question.

And at this point W. M. Simon quotes Paul Arbousse-Bastide, who is part of a contemporary redemptionist movement for Comte, as follows: "When a thinker has the curious privilege, in the eyes of posterity and particularly of his compatriots, of being held in both veneration and contempt we may be sure that, consciously or otherwise, he has put a fundamental question." Against such appreciation there has come from the pen of a British intellectual historian, Isaiah Berlin, an outrageous denunciation of Comte in a book on historical inevitability which leads one to conjecture whether Berlin has read Comte carefully or understood him at all.

What are some of the reasons for Comte's relegation to the museum of antiquities by contemporary sociologists and to the underworld of historical curiosa by some intellectual historians? First, as regards disciplines, Comte is in an ambivalent spot, ". . . a sociologist among philosophers and a philosopher among sociologists," as Raymond Aron puts it. The philosophers consider him to have been overambitious, and the sociologists consider him to be out of step with current research and with the refinements of the subject he formally founded. Each group of professionals sees him as a specialist in the field of the other. At that rate, we could also get rid of Leonardo da Vinci as being an inventor among painters and a painter among inventors, an act which would show how little we know about outstanding competence. Men of such competence do not fit easily into narrow academic niches known as subject matters and courses of study incorporated by college and university bureaucracies into what are called "departments," a word which appears to mean the result of separating one field of study from another, vain as such an endeavor always turns out to be. There is no more narrow mind than that of a "learned" scholar who cannot see the forest of man because of the misplanting of his own little deciduous foliage.

Second, Comte himself threw his ideas off their sociological track with his Religion of Humanity (discussed later in this book), which, in its attempt to set up a system of rituals, ceremonials, and fundamental emotional beliefs, drew into his camp all sorts of intellectual and religious eccentrics, who set up little positivist churches —sorry substitutes for what later came to be part of what is today an international, organized movement known as Humanism* which has numbered among its followers, Julian Huxley. Comte, thus, fell into disrepute among scholars and scientists by claiming that he had found the substitute for Christianity which modern science demanded. Early on, Thomas Huxley had taken a swipe at him, calling the Religion of Humanity "Catholicism minus Christianity" and in return being called "Pope Thomas" by Comte's self-appointed heirs.

Third, and highly important for explaining Comte's lack of influence in contemporary sociology, is the fact that he is not being read. Indeed, he does not seem to have been read deeply or at all even by writers of textbooks on the history of sociological thought. His works are not readily available though they have been translated into English. They can, moreover, be heavy going because the barbarous French he wrote is not easily put into non-turgid English except by paraphrasing such as was done in part by G. H. Lewes in 1853. Unfortunately, Lewes' book is based mainly on Comte's first multi-volume work on positive philosophy and not on the entire second multi-volume work, *System of Positive Polity*, which had not even fully appeared in French at the time of Lewes' translation. Today, we have Harriet Martineau's abridged translation of the *Cours de philosophie positive* and also a republication of the four-volume translation of the

* The delineation of contemporary Humanism can be found in the literature of the American Humanist Association and of the International Humanist Society.

Positive Polity, which ends with an appendix including all of Comte's early essays predating the *Cours*.

The two large works, the first abridged in English translation by Martineau and the second translated into English by various hands, serve well my purpose here of getting sociology back on the track established by Comte's contributions. I have drawn on them exclusively without reference to minor works. I have drawn up section and sub-section headings for my selections from Comte's major works which should give a rounded picture of his total schema. Some discussion of Comte's writings, excerpted from Lucien Lévy-Bruhl's excellent book on Comte, has also been included.

At the beginning of each section I have written a short essay seeking to put the topic concerned in perspective both as regards Comte's work in general and the specific significance of his ideas for their modern counterparts in particular. In short, I have sought to make it impossible for contemporary sociologists to be unaware of what we specifically and definitively owe to Comte by exposing students and scholars to the original sources and to a secondary source for which I have the highest regard. As the eminent British philosopher, Edward Caird, wrote:

A mind of such power cannot treat any subject without throwing much light upon it, which is independent of his special system of thought, and, above all, without doing much to show what are the really important difficulties in it which need to be solved. And, especially in such subjects, to discover the right question is to be half-way to the answer.

Finally, I cannot neglect quoting part of Lévy-Bruhl's concluding sentence in his book written fifteen years after Caird's: "The speculative philosophy of Comte is living still, and pursues its evolution even within the minds of those who are engaged in opposing it."

G. S.

New York City
January 1, 1969

Selected Bibliography in English

Comte's Own Works

1. AUGUSTE COMTE, The Positive Philosophy, freely translated and condensed by Harriet Martineau, New York: Calvin Blanchard, 1858.

2. AUGUSTE COMTE, System of Positive Polity, four volumes, London, 1875–77; reprinted, New York: Burt Franklin, 1966.

  a. First Volume, Containing the General View of Positivism and Introductory Principles, translated by John Henry Bridges, 1875.

  b. Second Volume, Containing Social Statics or The Abstract Theory of Human Order, translated by Frederic Harrison, 1875.

  c. Third Volume, Containing Social Dynamics or The General Theory of Human Progress, translated by Edward Spencer Beesly, Samuel Lobb, Fanny Hertz, John Henry Bridges, Vernon Lushington and Godfrey Lushington, 1876.

  d. Fourth and Last Volume, Containing the Synthetical Presentation of the Future of Man, with an Appendix consisting of Early Essays on Social Philosophy, translated by Richard Congreve and Henry Dix Hutton, 1877.

Books that Deal with Comte

1. RAYMOND ARON, Main Currents in Sociological Thought, vol. I, translated by Howard and Helen Weaver, New York: Basic Books, Inc., 1965; published in paperback, New York: Anchor Books, 1968. Pp. 59–105 are on Comte; other parts of the book are on Mon-

tesquieu, Marx, de Tocqueville, and the sociologists of the Revolution of 1848.

The well-known contemporary French sociologist's lucid analysis of Comte's work, based on copious knowledge and understanding, goes fairly deep. Aron shows rather conclusively that Comte's countrymen have today come to appreciate him highly.

2. EDWARD CAIRD, *The Social Philosophy and Religion of Comte*, Glasgow: James Maclehose and Sons (publishers to the University of Glasgow), 1885.

Caird, though an Hegelian, was very impressed by Comte; as a philosopher of religion and moral philosophy who was a believer as well, he was deeply appreciative of Comte's understanding that religion sought to deal with real problems of men even though not always successfully. It is significant that his stress is on the *System of Positive Polity* whereas Lévy-Bruhl tends to stress *The Positive Philosophy* and Aron sees them as a whole.

3. ROLLIN CHAMBLISS, *Social Thought, From Hammurabi to Comte*, New York: Holt, Rinehart and Winston, Inc., 1954.

Chambliss treats Comte in chapter 16, pp. 392–425.

4. F. J. GOULD, *Auguste Comte*, London: Watts and Co., 1920.

A book in a series called "Life-Stories of Great Men." I have had the use of a copy owned by the library of Brooklyn College of the City University of New York, which was originally Gould's own, in which he pasted all sorts of positivist tidbits and made handwritten notes and marginal comments, added pictures, and inserted at the end ten sonnets he wrote about Comte and positivism. The book is important as a manifestation of the kind of adoration still aroused by Comte in Britain even in the 1920's.

5. LUCIEN LÉVY-BRUHL, *The Philosophy of Auguste Comte*, translated by Kathleen de Beaumont-Klein with an introductory note by Frederic Harrison, New York: G. P. Putnam's Sons, 1903.

An excellent book largely based on the *Cours* which shows that Lévy-Bruhl had a profound understanding of the philosophical Comte, his permanent contributions, and his general importance as a thinker who has much to say to the twentieth century.

6. G. W. LEWES, *Comte's Philosophy of the Sciences: Being An Ex-*

position of the *Principles* of the *"Cours de philosophie positive"* of
Auguste Comte, London: Henry G. Bohn, 1853.
A good summary of the *Cours* though not strong on the socio-
logical side.

7. FRANK MANUEL, *The Prophets of Paris,* Cambridge, Massachusetts:
Harvard University Press, 1962; republished in paperback, New York:
Harper and Row, 1965.
The last chapter is on Comte and is preceded by chapters on
Turgot, Condorcet, St. Simon, and Fourier. I find Manuel's discus-
sion of Comte somewhat patronizing.

8. JOHN STUART MILL, *Auguste Comte and Positivism,* Ann Arbor:
University of Michigan Press, 1961.
A valuable paperback reprint of the famous British utilitarian
philosopher's two longish pieces on Comte: the first is on the *Cours,*
appreciative and on the whole laudatory; the second is on the *Posi-
tive Polity,* almost wholly condemnatory, particularly as regards
Comte's dogmatism and the "strange conceits . . . connected with
. . . M. Comte's frenzy for regulation."

9. F. S. MARVIN, *Comte,* London: Chapman and Hall, 1937.
A very disappointing book by a twentieth-century academic British
devoté of Comte that takes a long time to say very little.

10. W. M. SIMON, *European Positivism in the Nineteenth Century,
An Essay in Intellectual History,* Ithaca, N.Y.: Cornell University
Press, 1963.
A truly learned book which is not strong on sociology but very
informative on the battles that raged over Comte and positivism in
the nineteenth century. It contains a magnificent "Bibliographical
Appendix" and "Bibliography" proper, together covering almost a
hundred pages.

11. HERBERT SPENCER, *Reasons for Dissenting From the Philosophy of
M. Comte and Other Essays,* Berkeley, Calif.: The Glendessary Press,
1968.
Spencer's dissent was first published in 1864; second and third edi-
tions in 1870 and 1884. In 1914, it appeared in a book of Spencer's
essays. This 1968 reprint is a valuable contribution to scholarship in
sociology and the philosophy of science.

Contents

"The most conflicting schools of thought study the works of Auguste Comte and many ask: who is that man whose ideas appear to contain a clearer message to our generation than they did to his own?"

KATHLEEN DE BEAUMONT-KLEIN,
translator of L. Lévy-Bruhl's
The Philosophy of Auguste Comte.

"The science of man would be impossible if we were not able to get beyond our individuality, and to look at it, as well as at all other individualities, from the point of view of humanity."

EDWARD CAIRD,
The Social Philosophy and Religion of Comte.

Introduction

The sociology of Auguste Comte has become a classic. Too often, this ascription means that a man's work is revered but not intensively read, if read at all. One recent commentary even dispatches Comte with the curt announcement that if he had not founded sociology, somebody else would have come along about the same time and done so. This comment rests on the fatuous assumption that great systematic thinkers are always lying in wait to take their place in history. Thus, a seminal thinker is belittled as an accident of historical fortune and not seen as a creative formulator of new ideas stimulated by the climate of opinion of his time. At that rate, we could get rid of Moses, Jesus, Aquinas, Spinoza, Adam Smith, Karl Marx, and myriad other figures. In Howard Becker and Harry Elmer Barnes' massive three-volume Social Thought from Lore to Science, we find the following ambivalent views of Comte's work. First, they tell us that there was extremely little that was original in the theoretical content of Comte's work and that his main contribution was to give systematic form to a few of the somewhat detached and incoherent doctrines of his time. They accuse him of failing to absorb many of the most important developments of his time and of being behind the scientific achievements of his age in many ways. He was mainly a compendious encyclopedist, Becker and Barnes claim. Then, they turn tail and praise him for foreseeing the following modern trends: the "unity of science" movement; the development of the three "behavioral" sciences—anthropology, social psychology, and sociology; the stress on interdisciplinary research; the forging of deductive models of entire societies for the purpose of deriving heuristic hypotheses testable by computers. And to conclude their clumsy somersault,

1

they comment: "It may be said that Comte still haunts us; we are confronted by an old ghost with new sheets."

Comte himself, to be sure, in his later life did much to make some important thinkers of his time consider him a laughingstock. In regard to Comte's first great long work, Cours de philosophie positive, originally published in six volumes from 1830 to 1842, John Stuart Mill wrote that if Comte did not give us a full-blown sociology he at the very least made such a science possible by his work. But when, in a later work, Système de politique positive, originally published in four volumes from 1851 to 1854, Comte propounded his Religion of Humanity complete with priesthood, rituals, ceremonials, and worship, Mill was led to consider that a great mind had gone somewhat daft. In the 1840's, Mill had openly acknowledged Comte as one of the greatest men of the times. He reversed himself later when Comtean churches of the Religion of Humanity sprang up attracting some serious minds but also many strange characters. The churches have withered away in the twentieth century but their existence darkened Comte's reputation. Yet Comte's feeling for the great need of men for a system of beliefs is no longer considered as foolish as it originally seemed to some of his former admirers, and has something in common with the modern movement—Humanism. It was Comte's abracadabra of apparatus that made his religious movement look infantile and, indeed, a little preposterous.

Isidore Auguste Marie François Xavier Comte was born at Montpellier, France, in 1798, to a Catholic Royalist family. Hence, his early environment was counter-revolutionary. His life spanned the Napoleonic era, the Royalist Restoration including the bourgeois regime of Louis Philippe, the revolution of 1848, and the earlier years of the Second Empire. He was educated at the École Polytechnique in Paris where like a true young rebel he had trouble with the academic authorities. He was an excellent mathematician —which explains much of why he knew the restrictions on the use of mathematics—but his way in academic life was hard, as was true of other important sociological thinkers such as Karl Marx, Georg Simmel, and Comte's French follower, Emile Durkheim (during the early part of his career). It almost appears that in sociology there is a correlation between having academic difficulties as a young man and the development of important thinking later.

After being early drawn into the salon and circle of the vain, sparkling, and pecuniarily corrupt Claude-Henri de Rouvroy, Comte de Saint-Simon, Auguste Comte soon broke with him. Seemingly endless disputes have gone on and are still going on among anti-quarian scholars as to whether or not Comte stole all his leading ideas from Saint-Simon and merely expatiated on and systematized them. A reading of Saint-Simon's work, now made possible in a remarkable English translation by Felix Markham of his leading essays, will show that the shrewd surmises and epigrammatic sayings of Saint-Simon are merely a basis for the large works by Comte. Aquinas took ideas from Aristotle and Marx from Hegel. Each raised these ideas to a pinnacle far above where they were when first formulated.

Comte never held a high formal academic position although he was for a few years, from 1836 to 1846, an examiner at the École Polytechnique. Fired from that position, he lived on contributions from his religious disciples and admirers, including an American named Wallace who bequeathed him a small annuity for his later years. Comte had founded the Positivist Society in 1846. Eleven years later he died relatively unheralded by French academic life. His influence on academic French sociology was felt mainly through Emile Durkheim, and today Comte is considered a monumental figure in France. As usual with Frenchmen unjustly neglected during their lifetimes, a street in Paris was ultimately named after him.

Comte's intimate personal life was a disaster and is an intriguing subject for contemporary psychiatry. Twice he attempted suicide, both times in ways that would be detected and from which he would recover. Comte's self-image was, however, strong enough to enable him to continue to work and accomplish great things in spite of (or even, from one psychiatric point of view, because of) his deep psychic handicaps. Like all great humanitarians, at the level of the unconscious he must have hated humanity but sublimated his hatred through work and through seeking to lead men to establish a better society than the one in which he lived by basing it on love and benevolence. Thus, it was not for frivolous psychic reasons that he founded a Religion of Humanity and came to believe that his positivist philosophy and religion would appeal most strongly in the end to proletarians and to women (those who work and those whose work is insufficiently recognized). His deep-seated emotional difficulties and his contradictory internal dynamics do not in the least detract from his sociology and philosophy; indeed, they make his great achievements all the more remarkable. Intuitively, he saw the overwhelming import of emotion and instinct for social life.

This view becomes apparent when one examines his contributions to the then-budding science of psychology, where his insights are so acute that he borders on the discovery of the processes of the unconscious though he had no way of learning how it worked, the latter being Freud's contribution.

In an attempt to cover the spectrum of Comte's magistral contributions, I shall stress in this introduction the following topics: (1) the founding of a truly scientific sociology under the name of positivism; (2) the classification of the sciences and their interdependence of development; (3) the law of the three stages or states; (4) the sociology of science; (5) the sociology of knowledge; (6) sociology as comparative history; (7) social organism, social system, social structure, and social dynamics; (8) psychology and sociology; (9) sociological research methods: observation, experiment, and comparison; (10) the Religion of Humanity. In the selections from Comte in the main body of this book other topics will be treated as well.

Comte, as noted in my preface, wrote an abominable French and the English translations tend to read like Comte's French. W. M. Simon in his book on European positivism in the nineteenth century notes that Comte was the only French philosopher who wrote like a German one. Comte never claimed to be a littérateur and I cannot make him into one.

The founding of a truly scientific sociology under the name of positivism. By positivism, Comte in no sense meant a way of thinking that assured man complete certainty, but rather a way of connecting phenomena without recourse to supernatural or speculative causes. The chief characteristic of positive philosophy is its search for natural laws relative to the type of phenomena being studied in a science. In the grand historical process by which a subject matter becomes a science, obstacles have been met in every case. In no other case have the obstacles been so difficult to circumvent as in the forging of the new science of sociology or what Comte called "social physics."

Until the scientific method had been refined in the physical and biological sciences it could not be applied to the social sciences, since its worth had not yet been shown. Furthermore, for sociology to develop as a science it was necessary for man to have at his disposal material on a number of different societies so that through comparative observation he might discover what underlies all of them. There was no doubt in Comte's mind that such material had finally become available in his day as a result of the intellectual and international upheavals of the French Revolution which made clear the contrast between the new society and the older societies from which it sprang. The intellectual upheaval not only made it possible to begin forging a scientific sociology but made that sociology necessary for directing the course of technological innovation toward man's future welfare (see Chapter II, section 2 of this book).

Comte did not consider that he had discovered positivism as a way of thinking but rather that he was bringing it to its high point by applying it to the realm of social phenomena. Of earlier attempts made in this direction, Comte thought most highly in political theory of Aristotle's Politics and of Montesquieu's Spirit of the Laws. He also had some kind words for Condorcet and Hobbes, among others. But Comte did not seek anything so chimerical as the discovery of some general law that would subsume all phenomena of all science. The unity of science which he sought was the unity of the positivist method.

The progress of history is the story of the progress of the human mind in using the scientific method in all branches of learning, especially in sociology. Though sociology is the last of the sciences to appear in the great panoply of the development of the human mind, for Comte it turns out that the last shall be preeminent and that the only really universal point of view is the human or what Comte calls the social. Sociology for Comte dealt with the most particular, compound, concrete phenomena—those relative to man and his ability to live together with other men. Although Comte was not one to be preoccupied with definitions, at one point he described his goal as "the rational co-ordination of the fundamental sequence of the various events of human history according to a single design." Another quasi-definition implicit in Comte is that sociology is the science of the human mind whose development depends on human relationships. He also speaks of sociology as the search for the laws of social life.

Only sociology, for Comte, can achieve a generality of world view through which the seemingly heterogeneous physical and biological sciences can be shown to be united in their method. In his own words: "Imperfect as sociological study may yet be, it furnishes us with a principle which justifies and guides its intervention, scientific and logical, in all the essential parts of the speculative system, which can thus alone be brought into unity." Here in embryo is the sociology of science and the sociology of knowledge, for sociology makes possible "the rational cultivation of natural history" by showing how society is the indispensable condition and necessary aim of all the other sciences. The study of social and historical conditions will be seen as the true way to discover how and why developments occur in the other sciences.

The classification of the sciences and their interdependence of development. Classifications of the sciences had been made before Comte by men of considerable caliber. He was dissatisfied with all of them since they proceeded on the mistaken assumption that each science showed the development of a new or different human faculty, whereas the true problem was their interdependence and their inextricable continuity of development. In addition, lesser minds had established erroneous generalizations about the sciences as a whole through lack of sound knowledge of any of them.

Why was Comte so concerned with the classification of the sciences? For him, a positivistic classification of the sciences would really demonstrate how the human mind works at its rational best, and would regenerate education by showing the necessary interconnection of all the sciences. And most importantly for Comte, such classification would reveal that no social reorganization was possible until the homogeneity (but not uniformity) of scientific method could be shown to underlie all human knowledge.

Men seek to solve only such problems as those in power permit them to solve. The more the data of a science deal with the problems of man the greater the resistance of those in power to its prosecution. For science leads to action and action leads to change and change may lead as far as revolution. Moreover, the closer a science comes to studying man the more difficult is rational analysis, observation, experiment, and comparison regarding its data. For, as Comte wrote: "The most general and simple phenomena are the furthest removed from Man's ordinary sphere, and must thereby be studied in a calmer and more rational frame of mind than those in which he is more nearly implicated. . . ."

The sciences have developed chronologically in the following order: mathematics, astronomy, physics, chemistry, physiology, and social physics or sociology. Even the non-social sciences have met opposition during their development from the dominant political powers, and they have sometimes regressed. Subsequently, however, they have taken a new lease on life as power and technology changed hands and their interdependence with other sciences became clearer. The advancement of even the non-social sciences, though historically dependent on previously developed ones, is not assured simply by their prosecution; they must fight seemingly endless battles that grow more bitter as they come to cast illumination on the greatest science of all—sociology. Thus, to give an example from a time after Comte, the opposition to Darwinian biology arose most heatedly not from biologists but from theologians and spiritualist philosophers because the Darwinian conception of man as a primate threatened the bases of their social power. This last consideration leads us to the next topic of this introduction.

The law of the three stages or states. The three stages (or states) are the theological, the metaphysical, and the positive. Phenomena are observed and explained in the theological stage as productions of supernatural beings or divinities, and in the metaphysical stage as productions of abstract spiritualist forces (or to use the language of Sigmund Freud, by the omnipotence of thoughts which substitute psychic fantasies for realities). In the final or positive stage (which is not dead-end but dynamic), Comte writes, "The mind has given over the vain search after Absolute notions, the origin and destination of the universe, and the causes of phenomena, and applies itself to the study of their laws. . . . Reasoning and observation are the means of this knowledge." A sophisticated man, looking back over his life history, will see that he was a theologian in his childhood, a metaphysician in his youth, and a natural philosopher in his manhood. One may, moreover, be a positivist scientist in a given realm and think metaphysically or theologically in other realms. Nor does an earlier stage disappear from one realm of science because it is challenged by a later stage in another realm, but rather, attempts are made to assimilate positivist knowledge into the theological and metaphysical knowledge left over.

The three stages or states Comte enunciated do not inevitably succeed each other everywhere because there is progress in some area of science. The law of the three stages outlines the intellectual stations through which the human mind passes on its way to forging a science. One science may be in one stage, another in the second stage, and yet another in the third stage. And internally, each stage has its own dynamism. Stages overlap within each branch of science and among the sciences. Remnants of an earlier

stage may persist among certain strata of a population concerning
a science even though the positive stage has been achieved there
among its most eminent practitioners. Comte wrote:

During the whole of our survey of the sciences, I have endeavoured to
keep in view the great fact that all the three states, theological, metaphysical, and positive, may and do exist at the same time in the same
mind in regard to different sciences. . . . In the forgetfulness of it lies
the only real objection that can be brought against the grand law of the
three states. It must be steadily kept in view that the same mind may
be in the positive state with regard to the more complex and special;
and in the theological with regard to social science, which is so complex and special as to have hitherto taken no scientific form at all.

Comte here has anticipated the theory of primitive mentality later
developed by Lévy-Bruhl and then brought forcibly to the fore-
front of contemporary thought by psychoanalysis.

Comte's attack on the metaphysical mode of thought brought
howls of protest and derision from philosophers tied to the past.
To be sure, certain theological and metaphysical concepts and
modes of thought may be essential for a layman's emotional dilemmas. And thus, Comte's early heavy emphasis upon positivism as
the method of certainty for science appears to oversimplify certain
aspects of these human dilemmas. But he seems to have recognized
this overemphasis in his later work.

As has already been intimated, Comte well understood that the
positive stage, in sociology as in other sciences, was not stagnant or
static. As he wrote in his discussion of the new science of social physics
or sociology:

It would be absurd to pretend to offer this new science at once in a
complete state. Others, less new, are in very unequal conditions of for-
wardness. But the same character of positivity which is impressed on all
the others will be shown to belong to this. This once done, the philosophical condition of the modern will be in fact complete, as there
will then be no phenomenon which does not naturally enter into some
one of the . . . great categories [of sciences]. All our fundamental conceptions having become homogeneous, the Positive state will be fully
established. It can never again change its character, though it will be
forever in course of development by additions of new knowledge. Having acquired the character of universality which has hitherto been the
only advantage resting with the two preceding systems (theological
and metaphysical), it [the positive system] will supersede them by its
natural superiority, and leave to them only an historical existence.

This last over-optimistic assertion shows the strong utopian strain in Comte's thinking, a strain manifested concurrently by the utopian socialism that was beginning to make its appearance in Germany and France. As far as Comte is concerned, however, we may excuse his utopianism on the grounds of his frequent demonstration of realism and scientific encyclopedism. To judge a thinker only by his historically revealed errors is to lose perspective on how much we owe him for his truths.

The sociology of science. When we consider such aspects of what is today called the sociology of science as: (1) the general social conditions necessary to the growth of science; (2) the social role of the scientist; (3) the impediments to the growth of science; (4) the problems which science in general and special sciences in particular set for themselves—when we study these aspects as reflections of the state of society and culture—we cannot fail to see Comte as a preeminent thinker who early understood the significance of social factors to all sciences.

The revolution in science and in scientific method employed in formerly sacred subject matters is for Comte a fruit of the seventeenth century—of Bacon, Descartes, and Galileo. The theological class, which was set apart in the Middle Ages, itself set the stage for the seventeenth-century revolution. He writes: "Whatever might have been the confusion of intellectual labor, and the inanity of the leading investigations of the sacerdotal orders, it is not the less true that the human mind owes to them the first effectual separation between theory and practice, which could take place in no other manner." He follows this statement with:

Any spiritual expansion supposes the existence of a privileged class, enjoying the leisure indispensable to intellectual culture, and at the same time urged, by its social position, to develop to the utmost the kind of speculative activity compatible with the primitive state of humanity; and this description is answered by the sacerdotal institution established by the theological philosophy. . . . We must not forget that but for their activity in the days of its prime, human society would have remained in a condition much like that of a company of superior monkeys. By forming this speculative class, then, the theological philosophy fulfilled the political conditions of a further progression of the human mind.

The theological stage, however, proves its own undoing by failing to be able to settle the problems which arise in and through it and by the metaphysical problems which arise from it which cannot be answered by the existent theology. Though the metaphysical philosophy has its own dangers, intellectual and moral, it in turn raises questions which cannot be answered within the metaphysical orbit but only by beginning the systematic observation, comparison, and experimentation which lead into the stage of positivism. The theological stage when paramount is always contingent upon the supremacy of military regimes. The gods and the generals go hand in hand. The metaphysical stage is marked by religious and political upheaval whereas the positive stage is marked by the beginning of the supremacy of industry and technology.

Thus, Comte had already seen what latter-day historians began to see in recent decades: there was no "Dark Age" in western civilization, since opposition to theology and metaphysics was always being carried on somewhere, somehow, by the intellectual curiosity of the human mind for proof and evidence of the laws governing the universe and human life. One could even make a case for Comte's having seen the significance of the rise of what he calls "heretical Protestantism" for the growth of the positive spirit and of modern commerce and industry. The theory of the significance of the Protestant ethic for the rise of capitalism is not the discovery of Max Weber, as has been claimed.

Unlike Marx, Comte placed his faith in progress through the orderly permeation of the positive philosophy among common men and women rather than through a proletarian revolution. "Order and Progress" are Comte's mottoes, as opposed to "class struggle" and "the proletarian revolution." Yet, this stand which stresses "order" did not endear him to conservatives or reactionaries.

Comte's entire discussion of the effect of what he called "The Industrial Movement" on human personality, domestic life and the family; the abolition of the caste system; internationalism; industrial policy; Catholicism; administration; the growth of banking and public credit; the upsurge of invention (firearms, printing, maritime discovery); colonialism; slavery; and the flowering of the arts still deserves close reading despite the meandering, prolix style laden with repetition, and the uninviting character of his language.

The sociology of knowledge. In his essay summarizing the range of the sociology of knowledge in the book titled Modern Sociological Theory, Professor Franz Adler finds the major roots of this field in the Durkheim school of sociology, in Marx and the Marxists, in the anti-Marxists, especially Max Scheler and Paul

Honigsheim, and in Karl Mannheim. Comte is given less than scant treatment and is even treated as the parent of contemporary neo-positivism for which actually, as already noted, he has absolutely no responsibility at all except that the neo-positivists took over his title for their philosophy. When Comte talks about positivism, it cannot too often be stressed that he means an attitude of mind towards science and the explanation of nature, man, and society, and not some predilection for mathematical precision, especially not in sociology. In fact, Comte expressly makes a distinction between the search for certainty in science and the mistaken search for numerical precision.

Even the excellent book on the sociology of knowledge by Berger and Luckman, The Social Construction of Reality, makes no mention at all of Comte. Yet, from the standpoint of both the particular sciences and their ideologies, and the standpoint of ideology in general, Comte is the originator of the sociology of knowledge. The three leading general ideologies are for Comte, as one might expect, the theological, the metaphysical, and the positive. Comte realizes, like Marx and Engels, that "Social being determines social consciousness" not unilaterally but rather interdependently. Indeed, the whole aim of his positive philosophy is to help men develop a society in which "positivistic consciousness" determines social being—a society where if the scientist, especially the social scientist, is not king, at least every common man is to some degree a practitioner or respects the findings of social science. Even in a particular science where enough intellectual and methodological momentum has been gained inside the science itself to promulgate new problems and expand knowledge, it remains true that the science in its existent organizational state is interwoven with some general state of the society's fundamental beliefs and sentiments.

Max Scheler's distinctions between social conditions or what he calls "real factors," which do not determine knowledge but merely make it possible, and "ideal factors" where the succession of thought by new thought determines the state of knowledge, do not go as far as Comte's position. For Comte, social conditions determine whether a science can develop, to what degree it can develop, and the uses to which it can be put. Though the validity of propositions in knowledge may not be specifically determined by social conditions, the addiction to validity is itself determined by them. Once under way, the progress of positivist knowledge cannot be permanently stopped or pushed back, but neither can it continue to advance without social conditions adequate to the intellectual needs of its adherents.

As for ideologies in general, men of primitive power pursue theological thinking because they need it to retain their dominance in social life and to keep other men in subjection. Only long struggles for positivistic ideology by men of foresight serve to achieve social conditions under which metaphysical propositions give way to positivistic ones. Conversely, the positivistic stage is reached in any science—and especially in sociology—through a continual reorganization of society made possible by the pursuit of sociology and its application to practical problems, particularly problems in the organization of knowledge, its propagation, and its being passed on from generation to generation. Thus, Jean Lacroix is correct in his little book, La Sociologie d'Auguste Comte, published in Paris in 1956, when he writes that in the final analysis positivism is essentially a pedagogy.

Neither here under the heading of the sociology of knowledge nor in other parts of sociology is it my intent to start a "back to Comte" movement in sociology like the ill-fated "back to Kant" movement in philosophy but rather to suggest the feasibility of a "forward with Comte" movement by pushing ahead with the implications of his thought. But to push ahead, his thoughts must be known and must once again become coins of the sociological realm.

Sociology as comparative history. Comte is often treated as if his chief contribution were to the philosophy of history, and he has indeed been called the French Hegel. But Comte was interested in the study of history primarily as a basis for discovering the laws governing the social organism, social structure, and social dynamics. History is a laboratory for the sociologist in that it enables him to compare different types of society, to discover their common elements, and to account for the differences in their structure and in their dynamic flow.

Why did the old patterns of western society break down and wither away and give rise to modern industrial society? This question is basic to Comte's development of sociology, and in answering it, he refuses to become bogged down in historical minutiae. What Comte is looking for are the laws of social existence, and he writes:

We must avoid confounding the abstract research into the laws of social existence with the concrete histories of human societies, the explanation of which can result only from a very advanced knowledge of the whole of these laws. Our employment of history in this inquiry, then, must be essentially abstract. But the laws of social existence cannot be discovered until the entire system of the preceding sciences has been formed, and the whole mass of historical information offered as material for its analysis. The function of Sociology is to derive, from this mass of unconnected material, information which, by the principles of the biological theory of man, may yield the laws of social life.

The scientific comparison of immutable landmarks throughout the whole of past human experience will afford a direction and a rallying point for sociology, and will reveal the fundamental structure of all societies, the reasons for the peculiarities of each, and the goals for social reorganization which modern sociology can posit for man. Modern institutions are not all suitable to man's needs and their adaptation can be achieved only by understanding the irrelevancy of certain theologically and metaphysically based institutions to the positive spirit of modern industrialism. Here is contained a first intimation of the concept of anomy that Durkheim enunciated at the end of his work in 1893 on the division of labor in society, a concept which Durkheim himself indicated was not his own discovery but rather an expatiation on Comte's theme.

For almost a century Comte has been the butt of bad jokes by sorry historical academicians. Thus, there is more than poetic justice, there is scientific justice, in the recent discovery of the importance of sociological considerations to the understanding of history as a subject. We now attempt to bring to life even the most minute of historical events by showing them in the context of the type of society in which they occur and their concurrence or discordance with other elements of existing institutions and orders of social relationships. Thus, the French Revolution, which brought down the old order and ushered in the new, was not simply a political or economic phenomenon but the result of massive disjunctions among the various segments of the old society. Were Comte alive today he might point to the Russian and Chinese Revolutions as proof of what happens when a weary ideological order impedes the forces of material and intellectual progress which are impinging upon it. Comte had an intellectual quality sadly lacking among too many contemporary American sociologists: learned vision.

For the fact-burdened peddler of history, the historicist, history consists of unique events, but for Comte it consists of a laboratory for research into the general trends and tendencies of whole societies. In fact, one might go so far as to say that, for Comte, unique events when thoroughly investigated are not unique at all. Comte's sociology is societal, not a series of isolated monographs on specific subjects or compartments studied in isolation. It is the search for human perfectability and not a disembodied discipline far above the madding crowd and impervious to the vital impact of new technology, new administrative techniques, the rise of social classes, and the struggle for power among discordant factions. A new elite of men of learning, each pursuing his appointed task, yet under the aegis of sociology as a manifestation of their mutual interdependence, would also be pursuing the general positive philosophy and make possible human progress never before contemplated.

It is easy to accuse Comte of grand historical generalizations by failing to realize that we all have to live by some such generalizations. He had the unmitigated courage to spell out the details of these generalizations and what they boded for the future. He also saw the necessity that such generalizations be openly arrived at. Open generalizations openly arrived at—not secret, undigested generalizations covertly guiding specific little pieces of research—were the aim and goal of the new science which he named and sociologists today pursue, though generally not in the manner he intended. Comte was not a mediocre theorist but a genius who took in the large overall view, and like all geniuses he often, to be sure, overstepped the boundaries of his otherwise good sense.

Social organism, social system, social structure, and social dynamics. Long before late nineteenth-century sociologists began to discuss the concept of society as an organism and years before Darwin propounded his theories, Auguste Comte hit upon the idea of conceiving society as an organism. Thus, the idea of a "social system," which gave such notoriety to the American Talcott Parsons and his cohort of terminological enthusiasts, is already presaged in Comte. He uses the term "social organism" to describe society as a consensus of parts, an interconnection of institutions similar to the interconnection of functions in an organism. He does not reach the absurd lengths of certain later nineteenth-century and even early twentieth-century sociologists who by argument from analogy found all parts of living organisms existing in society, to the point where Brunschwig found the church to represent the female sex and the state the male sex. Comte feels no science could ever be explained wholly through argument by analogy. He understands that each science has its own subject matter which inevitably leads to investigation of new phenomena by newly appropriate methods, and he holds to the self-subsistent character of every science internally even though externally its further development depends upon the state of society and the supremacy of the positivist doctrine in philosophy. He uses the term "social system" to describe the subject of social statics which, he writes, "consists in the investigation of the laws of social action and reaction of the different parts of the social system." Comte writes further that, "The scientific principle of the relation between the political and the social condition is simply this—that there must always be a spontaneous harmony between the whole and the parts of the social system, the elements of which must inevitably be, sooner or later, combined in a mode entirely conformable to their nature." This mutual interaction, however, is not always harmonious. Lack of harmony in the functioning of parts will result in change or even upheaval. This idea leads to Comte's discussion of the two main fields of sociology—social statics and social dynamics.

Social statics is concerned with the study of social organization. But social organization must be looked at as a totality. Comte writes:

There can be no scientific study of society, either in its conditions or its movements, if it is separated into portions, and its divisions are studied apart. . . . Materials may be furnished by the observation of different departments; and such observation may be necessary for that object, but it cannot be called science. The methodical division which takes place in the simple inorganic sciences is thoroughly irrational in the recent and complex science of society and can produce no results. The day may come when some sort of subdivision may be practicable and desirable; but it is impossible for us now to anticipate what the principle of distribution may be; for the principle itself must arise from the development of the science; and that development can take place not otherwise than by the formation of the science as a whole. The complete body will indicate for itself, at the right season, the particular points which need investigation; and then will be the time for such special study as may be required. . . . It is no easy matter to study special phenomena in the only right way—viewing each element in the light of the whole system. It is no easy matter to exercise such vigilance so that no one of the number of contemporary aspects shall be lost sight of. But it is the right and the only way; and we may perceive in it a clear suggestion that this lofty study should be reserved for the highest order of scientific minds, better prepared than others, by wise educational discipline, for sustained speculative efforts, aided by an habitual subordination of the passions to the reason.

Sociology, for Comte, is a dynamic study in two senses: it will change the conditions of man in society through social reorganization and it is itself the study of how social changes necessarily take place as interrelated structures and functions break down and require rearrangement. Social dynamics cannot be adequately understood without knowledge of what he calls the spontaneous order of human society or social statics. The basic social elements whose study make up social statics are: (1) the instinctual and emotional make-up of man's biological and psychological existence; (2) religion as regulative; (3) property and material life; (4) the family as the basic unit of social organization based upon the sexual and parental relationships; (5) language whose origin is familial and whose development is social in the broader sense; (6) large-scale social organizations or secondary groups, which are economic (through the distribution of employments) and governmental; (7) social existence seen as a whole; (8) the limits of variation within social statics.

All these elements are subject to the dynamic workings of society through change and progress. And although they make society possible, analyses of these static elements do not give us the clue to the true heart of sociology, the study of social dynamics or what Comte calls the theory of the natural progress of human society. The causes for the dynamism inherent in man's social situation involve climate, physical environment, population growth through an increased birth rate and a decreased mortality rate, technology, the steady advancement of science from the theological to the positivist stage, and the growth of law and civilian government. Thus, Comte is led into detailed analyses of the whole pageant of western history, arriving finally at the notion that our "present confusion" can be resolved only by a new morality based upon the benevolent political philosophy of positivism which will give wise systematic direction to the next great movement in human progress.

Psychology and sociology. The famous early American sociologist Lester F. Ward, who was known for his strict scientific scruples and who rarely indulged himself by failing to understand the work of other thinkers, nevertheless made an egregious error by holding Comte's sociology to be grounded in an inadequacy of psychology. Ward was far off the mark here. The difficulty probably arose because Comte, as far as possible, avoided use of the term "psychology". The unhappy term he uses is "cerebral biology" and he severely criticizes most of what was called psychology in his time as incapable of being a science. He sees the importance of studying the relations of the affectual states of man to his intellectual faculties but does not consider that to be psychology, although, as we shall see, his discussion throughout on this relationship is psychologically accurate to the point of being a forerunner of certain contemporary thinking. Comte propounds some very general ideas on psychology or cerebral biology as a science which have striking analogues in psychoanalysis, the psychology that has revolutionized man's concept of himself. His early British follower, G. H. Lewes, wrote in 1853: "Positive philosophy . . . if not in a condition, as yet, to elaborate a science of psychology . . . clears the way for one, by pointing out the direction which investigation must take." That direction was not forthrightly taken until a half-century later when Freud came to put flesh on the bare bones of Comte's affectual psychology.

The Enlightenment enthroned Reason—a well-nigh disembodied Reason—as the criterion of judgment concerning the worth of a human society. Comte certainly was not a child of this Enlightenment. He begins his own psychological discussion with a searching criticism of Descartes for falling into the trap of the rationalistic fallacy. Comte deeply appreciated the "glorious service" rendered by Descartes in mathematics and physics. But in psychological matters Descartes retreated, in Comte's view, to theological and metaphysical stages by representing man as a reasoning animal. For all his immense belief in man's being capable of modification and improvement in his social relations through intellect and reason (that is, through being guided by positivistic thinking), Comte saw, nevertheless, that it is the human instincts which are paramount originally and which remain basic to the flowering of intellect and reason themselves. Here is a foreshadowing of Freud's view that the unconscious and the instincts are the foundation of all human mental energy with their most ennobling derivatives being science, art, and abstract thought. Says Comte:

The affections, the propensities, the passions, are the great springs of human life. . . . Their spontaneous and independent impulse is indispensable to the first awakening and continuous development of the various intellectual faculties, by assigning to them a permanent end, without which—to say nothing of their general direction—they would

remain dormant in the majority of men. It is even but too certain that
the least noble and most animal propensities are habitually the most
energetic, and therefore the most influential.

The separation of instinct from reason is for Comte a throwback to
the metaphysical mode of thinking. Human nature is induced in
various directions by distinct and independent powers, among which
equilibrium is established with extreme difficulty. Here again is a striking similarity to Freud's view of the interplay of id, ego, and superego.
Yet Freud knew almost nothing about Comte's systematic work. Even
Comte's insight in his work on positive polity, that dreams show
the preponderance of the affective faculties over the intellectual
faculties, is not mentioned in Freud's presumably exhaustive history
in the first chapter of The Interpretation of Dreams.

Comte followed hard upon the heels of the psychological theories
of Franz Joseph Gall, the founder of phrenology, which was then a
respectable subject seeking to topographically chart out areas of the
brain in order to establish where specific human faculties and character traits had their seat. Phrenological topography never worked out
and this false trail led Comte somewhat astray.

The new science of sociology, wrote Comte, is rooted in biology.
Everybody, he notes, seems willing to agree to this statement and
then goes about neglecting it in practice. Comte thinks this neglect
arises from the most conspicuous defect of biological science—
failure to deal adequately with intellectual and moral phenomena—
and goes about seeking to rectify it. When finally this imperfection
is removed, cerebral biology or psychology will be able to provide
the starting point of all social speculation, in accordance with the
analysis of the social faculties of man and of the organic conditions
which determine their character. But sociology is more than psychology for Comte. From psychology, sociology learns to understand
the agents of collective phenomena and then shows how the social
environment affects the workings of the instincts and determines
the course of human progress in history.

In Positive Polity, Comte amplified his ideas on psychology,
stressing once again the predominance of the emotive over the merely
intellectual functions. Here he divides emotional life into the personal and the social; the personal side Comte calls "egoism," the
social side, "altruism." This second term was later taken over by
Herbert Spencer, who, in a most unusual act, acknowledged his debt
to Comte. Egoism and altruism, for Comte, are in permanent con-

flict—an idea which contains another basic tenet of psychoanalysis, the clash of narcissism with social demands on the individual.

For Comte there are three sets of instincts: personal, intermediate, and social. The personal are the instinct of self-preservation, the sexual instinct, the maternal instinct, the aggressive instinct, and the industrial instinct. The last sounds peculiarly like the instinct of workmanship proclaimed by Thorstein Veblen seventy-five years later in his book by that name. The intermediate instincts are pride (love of power) and vanity (love of approbation). The social instincts are attachment to other human beings, veneration or voluntary submission, and benevolence.

The types of individual character which emerge in social life are principally determined by the constitution of the emotional area of human life. The latter's development, in turn, depends upon the influences exerted by the intellectual and moral faculties which are themselves reflections of the social statics and dynamics pervasive in a given society. Yet, human will, no matter how it is socialized, is the acting out of desire after mental deliberation has decided on the propriety of some predominant impulse—a prevision of the psycho-analytic doctrine of rationalization. Though intellectual functions inspire special desires, they are deficient in the energy necessary to induce action which depends solely on the emotional impulse.

Sociological research methods: observation, experiment, and comparison. Discussion of the scientific methodology proposed by Comte for sociology will place it within the general perspective of his total doctrine, show that the view that Comtean sociology is antagonistic to contemporary research methods in sociology is mistaken, and reveal how really "modern" and even "contemporary" his methodology was. In short, Comte is not a part of a bygone intellectual tradition which gives sociologists a past to wallow in; he is part and parcel of valuable intellectual baggage they carry around today.

According to Comte, two main methods are available to social physics or sociology: direct methods which are peculiar to the subject itself and indirect methods which draw materials from other sciences and incorporate them into the subject's direct methods. The direct methods are: (1) observation, (2) experiment, (3) comparison.

In the use of observation, the first problem is to develop ways and means of assuring that different sociologists will be able to see, hear, and experience the same phenomena. Observation of such a uniform kind cannot be assured unless it takes place on the basis of established sociological laws, no matter how elementary they are at the beginning. Without laws and the testing of hypotheses based upon them, we would amass a scattering of random observations. Comte writes, "Social science requires, more than any other, the subordination of observation to the statical and dynamical laws of phenomena. No social fact can have any scientific meaning till it is connected with some other social fact; without such connection it remains a mere anecdote, involving no rational utility." Attention must be called here to the fact that Durkheim lifted this last idea bodily from Comte in his own Rules of Sociological Method a half-century later and that with majestic invalidity Durkheim has since been credited with being its author.

At first, Comte continues, good observers will be rare because they cannot systematize their observations through laws and hypotheses but this situation will improve as the science develops. This shortcoming has its good side since it will keep petty minds from meddling with this most difficult subject. A mind suitably trained in scientific method becomes able to convert almost all impressions from the events of life into sociological data when experience is combined with an innate talent to interrelate them.

When Comte comes to the discussion of experimentation in sociological research, he distinguishes with unerring vision the use of both "natural experiments," as John Stuart Mill called happenings in history, over which the sociologist has no control but which he uses as data and "artificial experiments" or what are today thought of as "controlled experiments."

Employing indirect methods of experimentation in observation of diseased states of the social organism, Comte demonstrates a keen appreciation of the use of the so-called abnormal for the discovery of the normal—a project which Durkheim has for long been credited with systematically initiating and which Freud used to such magnificent advantage in arriving at an approximation of a normal ego. Comte's discussion of this topic contains the kernel of one aspect of the idea of anomy and also supports Freud's belief that a singular case could often be found to be typical of a whole range of cases and make continuous replication unnecessary.

In his discussion of the use of comparison as part of scientific method in sociology, Comte begins by pointing out the great value of comparing whatever rudiments of social life we find among the lower animals with that found among humans—a method which later was for a time much in vogue and was used in studies made of the social life of ants, bees, and the lower primates. Comte thought the first germs of social relations could be discovered among the lower animals, and this method has since proven of some advantage in such subsidiary fields of sociological study as the family, the division of labor, and the socialization process. In a revolutionary statement, he points out that the discovery of man's relation to the lower animals will do much to undermine what he calls the "insolent pride" of the ruling classes who consider themselves a special species above mankind. With modesty, he concludes that since he can as yet offer only the first conception of a science of sociology, he can himself make little use of this kind of comparison, but this inability on his part only underlines the necessity to point it out lest its omission should hamper the advancement of the subject he was founding. Comte was already stressing man's similarities to the lower animals years before Darwin spelled out his laws of biological evolution.

The chief use Comte sees of the method of comparison is the discovery—through the study of coexisting states of society in different parts of the world—of social structures, social classes, social functions, and those patterns of social behavior which are universal. "The human mind," he writes, "is uniform in the midst of all diversities of climate, and even of race, such diversities having no effect upon anything more than the rate of progress." Still, comparison of coexisting societies will not give us the chief scientific tool of positive sociology: the comparison of consecutive stages through which society passes. Here the historical method of comparison is paramount. Our existing state cannot be understood simply through study of it as it is, but only by seeing it as part of the series of social states from which it has emerged and which have left their imprint upon our minds. Every law of social succession disclosed by the historical method must be unquestionably connected, directly or indirectly, with the positivist theory of human nature already discussed here under the heading of Comte's view of psychology. Thus, the main strength of sociological demonstrations must ever lie in the concordance of the conclusions of historical analysis with the preparatory conceptions of the psychobiological theory. This part of the method of comparison, the historical method, will enable us to analyze the most complex phenomena by seeing them in the light of their development. And thus we find, Comte tells us, a confirmation of the chief intellectual character of the new science—the philosophical preponderance of the spirit of the whole over the spirit of detail.

A few last words by Comte on method are in order here since they relate conspicuously to the present penchant for mathematical exactitude. They go as follows: "The most perfect methods may, however, be rendered deceptive by misuse and this we must bear in mind. We have seen that mathematical analysis itself may betray us into substituting signs for ideas, and that it conceals inanity of conception under an imposing verbiage."

The Religion of Humanity. Comte's Positive Polity spells out the positivist religion which came to serve as the Bible for a rather odd collection of worshippers. Despite his attempt to replace all existing beliefs, customs, and conventions by new names, Comte's bizarre religion still retained old ideas and sentiments. Thus, the little French boy who had early broken away from Catholicism and denounced the theological method of thought (but not religion) wound up by founding a church of his own.

His church, founded on the Religion of Humanity, was a strange concoction. Sociologists were to be its priests. They were to be the scientific directors of society and to interpret the positivist doctrine of love, order, and progress. The positivist priests were not to exercise political power but to influence opinion through education and preaching. The common man, imbued with the positivist philosophy, would thus be able to evolve a most enlightened public opinion. This common man would be a proletarian. The future belonged to the intelligent workingman, not through losing his chains but through improving his positivistic brains. Comte was seeking to compensate men for the God and the universal (Catholic) church that positivism and sociology must necessarily take from them. He also feared the triumph of the military and distrusted professional politicians although some of his political views, especially regarding the Revolution of 1848 and the Second Empire, were extremely naïve. If he did not expect that all men would, through positivism, become quickly altruistic, he at least hoped that a form of secular worship would help them become less egoistic. But he finally went so far as to develop a messianic complex in which he saw himself as a Moses leading his positivist children out of the wilderness of theology and metaphysics to a land flowing with milk, honey, and sociology. It sounds like premature senility unless one tears away the elaborate trappings and sees underneath them the sublimations of his love of mankind, his hatred of cruelty, and his worship of women.

There is a school of thought in France which holds that there is no inherent contradiction between the scientific Comte who founded sociology, classified and interrelated the sciences, and propounded the law of the three stages, and the later Comte who founded the Religion of Humanity since, it is claimed, in both cases his ruling passion was the betterment of man. Comte was not willing to accept the possibility that a strong sense of selfhood could be sufficiently established in men without rites, ceremonials, daily worship, and collective institutions such as his new religion demanded and without a new universal group such as his positivist church.

In the commentaries at the head of each section and in Comte's own words, ideas in this introduction will be clarified further.

1

The Practical Philosophical Problem Facing Comte

A revolution takes decades, even centuries in some cases, to thread its way through the social labyrinth. Properly understood, the term betokens a process through which men's conception of themselves undergoes change, and coercive power and economic control are reallocated. It is usually erroneously taken to refer to the event of armed insurrection, which is only the most spectacular part of the total process.

The consolidation of a revolution through new general beliefs and sentiments in the population at large marks its accomplishment. Until this consolidation takes place, the myths of the past ebb and flow even as their underlying philosophy is subverted. The insurrectionary stage of the French Revolution, the great revolution which permeated all of western Europe, led to civil war against the old regime, to internecine strife among the insurrectionists, to foreign intervention, and then to the factitious restoration of monarchy under Napoleon. Napoleon's self-made dynasty was held together by concessions to the Catholic Church, the liberalization and expansion of civil law, and distraction of the populace with foreign wars. After the fall of Napoleon from power, some of the broad changes begun in 1789 remained, but the foundations of social relationships were shaky and unstable. A renaissance in Catholic social theory and in royalist ideology took place along with the rise of the bourgeoisie on the land and in the towns and the emergence of industrialists in factory and mill. Talleyrand and his mid-European ally, Metternich, addicted to the ideals of the old regimes, compromised the revolution's ideals of the Rights of Man—liberty, equality, and fraternity

—and pursued a wobbly path in support of a nobility which, true to the traditions of the Bourbons, "had learned nothing and forgotten nothing."

Despite the earlier turmoil and the presumably chastened restoration of "legitimate" authority under monarchical auspices in 1815, women and children, particularly among the common people, remained in cruel subjection. For their part, the physical and biological sciences continued to forge ahead with ineluctable momentum on by-roads far from the path of the new apologetics of the more dogmatic Catholic thinkers and circumventing the citizenry whose elders had been called to arms in 1789.

How, then, could the revolution be consolidated? Counterrevolution seemed to have won the day. Where could the common men and women who had staked their destinies on republicanism turn for guidance in a culture rent asunder with regard to the Roman Catholic Church, run by a privileged few and disdainful of the "revolutionary rabble"? Where could they find an answer to their deepest emotional concerns? For Auguste Comte, this practical problem, which had been ardently discussed among the Saint-Simonians, could only be met by a new philosophical orientation. In 1822, at the age of twenty-four, he daringly sought to spell out "A Plan for Reorganizing Society." This work turned out to be a prevision of things to come from his pen.

At this early stage, Comte placed his hopes for a reorganization of social relationships upon a rather restricted elite but subsequently he came to feel that positivist education of workers and of women would widen this elite. Yet, Comte's later educational ideals led him into a bureaucratic rigidity in the inculcation of beliefs and sentiments which was at variance with the spontaneity of emotional life stressed so much in his psychology. This rigidity arose in no small part from his "organic" attitude concerning society, stressing consensus rather than a balance of conflicting interests and tending to see anarchic disorder wherever there was disequilibrium. In this regard, Emile Durkheim was also led astray when he labelled disequilibrium "anomy." But fortunately, disequilibrium and anomy always exist; it is equilibrium and lack of anomy that threaten to stifle spontaneity.

Comte never saw the mature development of democratic institutions containing their own dynamism of welfare and legal protection of the basic rights of individuals. It is significant that modern French government, which was initiated by the revolutionary movement (the "spirit of '89" as it has been called), has consistently tried to stifle the same basic rights which brought forth thinkers who stressed the humanitarian ideals underlying them.

1. *The Philosophical Problem*

According to Comte, philosophy is destined to serve as a basis for morality, for politics and for religion. . . .

Comte is going to endeavour to reorganise beliefs, that is to say, to substitute a demonstrated faith to the revealed faith whose force is now spent. This demonstrated faith will have nothing in common with the natural religion of the XVIII. century, which was at bottom but a weak and degenerate form of belief in the supernatural. Under the metaphysical garb of Deism we still recognise theological thought. On the contrary the demonstrated faith will have its origin and its justification in positive science. The two words "faith" and "demonstration" appear to clash with each other. But the contradiction lies merely on the surface. For we are still concerned with "faith" since the great majority of men will always have to take on faith the conclusions of positive philosophy.

The number of men with sufficient leisure and enough culture to examine these conclusions and to go into their proofs will always be small. The attitude of the others must be one of submission and respect. But, differing on this point from the religious dogmas which humanity has known until now, the new faith will be "demonstrated." It will contain nothing which has not been established and controlled by scientific methods, nothing which goes beyond the domain of the relative, nothing which at any moment cannot be proved to a mind capable of following the demonstration.

This form of "faith" already exists in the case of a great number of scientific truths. . . .

Faith therefore signifies here not indeed a voluntary abdication of the intellect in presence of a mystery which surpasses its power of comprehension, but a submission to fact, which in no way encroaches upon the rights of reason. Every man is not capable, at any moment, of exercising this right to criticise. In practice, Comte will

SOURCE: Lévy-Bruhl, *The Philosophy of Auguste Comte*, pp. 23–24, 26–27, 29–30, 34.

severely restrict the use of it. But in theory this right belongs to all men, and must ever remain unalterable. . . .

If, therefore, a society be a prey to chronic disorders, which political remedies appear powerless to cure, one has every right to believe that the deep-rooted evil has its origin in intellectual disorganisation. All other troubles are merely symptoms. This, according to Comte, is precisely the state of contemporary society. . . .

Does not this state represent the ordinary condition of human societies? Perhaps the "organic" state only appears occasionally and as an exception? Such a supposition is groundless. For, if such were the case societies could not subsist, and above all could not develop. We must admit, on the contrary, that periods of intellectual anarchy form the exception, and that in a normal state of society men are united by their unanimous submission to a sufficiently large body of principles and beliefs. History confirms this view. . . .

The problem of the organisation of beliefs would seem to come under two heads. In the first place we have the philosophical problem: how to establish a system of principles and beliefs capable of being universally admitted; and, in the second place, a social problem: how to bring all minds into the new faith. But this distinction only appears on the surface. As a matter of fact, the solution of the first problem will necessarily imply that of the second. . . .

Now, up to the present time, the positive mode of thought has not shown itself in a position to respond to this demand. It has only produced individual sciences. Positive Science has been "special" and fragmentary, always attached to the investigation of a more or less restricted group of phenomena. . . .

In the present state of things, the positive mind is "real" but "special." The theologico-metaphysical mind is "universal" but "fictitious." We can neither sacrifice the "reality" of science, nor the "universality" of philosophy. Which is the way out of this difficulty?

Three solutions alone are conceivable:

1. To find a reconciliation which will make it possible for the two modes of thought to coexist without contradiction:

2. To re-establish unity by making the theologico-metaphysical method universal:

3. To re-establish unity by making the positive method universal. . . .

Since the conciliation between the positive mode of thought and the other one is impossible; since the exclusive ascendency of the theologico-metaphysical mode of thought is out of the question;

since when all is said the human mind needs a philosophy, it follows
that that philosophy can only proceed from the positive mode of
thought itself. There is nothing, a priori, to prevent this solution
from being realised. For the last positions of the theologico-metaphysical spirit are surely not impregnable. This spirit, "fictitious" in
its essence, never could become "real." The positive spirit is only
accidentally "special." It is quite capable of acquiring the universality
which it lacks. The new philosophy would then be founded, and the
problem of perfect logical coherence would be solved.

The whole difficulty thus appears to be in "universalising" the
positive mode of thought. To do this it must be extended to those
phenomena which are still habitually conceived according to the
theologico-metaphysical mode, that is to say, to the moral and social
phenomena. This will be Comte's crowning discovery. He will found
"social physics." By so doing he will take from theology and metaphysics the last reason of their existence. He will make possible the
transition from a positive science to an equally positive philosophy.
Thus will be realised "the unity of the understanding," and this
mental harmony will carry with it as its consequence the moral and
religious harmony of humanity.

2

Forerunners of and Conditions for Sociology as a Positive Science

Comte had great respect for Aristotle and for certain thinkers of the eighteenth century but he evinced no great admiration for the overwhelming majority of social thinkers of the two millennia between, seeing in them mainly expatiation of theological and metaphysical principles.

For the political economists, Comte had little sympathy. They separated economics from sociology, and in so doing, they became preoccupied with problems of production and consumption without regard to their involvement in social philosophy. In addition, by stressing individual liberty of enterprise they failed to see that its pursuit must lead to social anarchy. Thus, Comte foresaw the growth of what became institutional economics as first promoted by Thorstein Veblen in the United States at the end of the nineteenth century. For one political economist, Adam Smith, Comte had the highest regard. This regard is to be expected since Smith was a moral philosopher (indeed, he held the chair of moral philosophy at the University of Glasgow). To Adam Smith, economics was a science of material wealth, but only as it related to total human welfare. Yet, despite his criticism of a majority of economists, Comte (true to his doctrine of historical relativism which saw men in the context of their times) understood that they had put an end to medieval theologizing concerning economic life and to the mercantilism that preceded modern economic institutions.

As for those who sought patterns in history in order to make it the basic social science, Comte evinces great respect, especially for Bossuet. But he finds this search so metaphysically grounded that it cannot achieve scientific status and he is, thus, further convinced

29

of the necessity for the new science of sociology which will incorporate history and the historical method into its search for laws of human organization and development.

A science concerned with social relationships could come into being only when scientific method and scientific principles were already being used to explain the heavens, the earth, the elements, and organisms. Rational explanation of the inorganic and organic worlds precedes rational explanation of man and his relations with his fellows. But science forges ahead concurrently with changes in the foundations of political power.

The science of social physics or sociology becomes possible when the mass of men assert their rights as human beings. In asserting these rights they flounder, fall back, resurge, and seek anew. As they seek for new principles to live by, men tend to take two steps forward and one step backward as their search is compromised by "retrograde" (outdated) and "negative" (nihilistic) principles. But finally their conception of themselves as citizens of a nation steeled by revolution and, indeed, as citizens of the world is climaxed by the emergence of the science of sociology which is premised upon the ability of man to view himself as a scientific phenomenon and as a being endowed with the special privilege of civic morality. This new conception—the practical condition for positivist sociology—arises from the emancipation of women; the abolition of slavery; the scientific breakthroughs of the sixteenth, seventeenth, and eighteenth centuries; the growth of urban industry arising from modern technology (which creates an industrial class of employers at odds with feudal landlords with a caste system rooted in hereditary nobility); the accompanying rise of the industrial working class; the rise of individualistic art forms, the secular nation-state, changes in the clergy; the rise of law; the growth of logic through science; and finally the confirmation of this very conception through the establishment of positivist sociology. Sociology breaks down the distinction between theory and practice since the theory leads to action and action gave rise to the theory. This ultimate pragmatism of positivism, significantly, parallels the doctrines of Karl Marx and Friedrich Engels, seen particularly in their thesis that the aim of pre-existing philosophy had been to explain the world, whereas what was needed was a philosophy that sought to change it.

In his later writings, Comte comes to the conclusion that the revolution of 1789 laid the basis for common men to understand that their emotions need to be left untrammeled by pseudo-moralities which inhibit their instincts for love, security, and intellectual and aesthetic growth. But to keep the inherent vigor of instinctual life from leading to social anarchy, positivism (with sociology as its keystone) must become a faith having followers and interpreters. Then sociology will become the means through which humanity, newly arisen from the ashes of the old regime, can fulfill its deepest hopes.

Comte staked out his claim in positivist sociology with such verbosity and encyclopedic pretensions that he nearly blotted out his own insights with redundancy. Rarely does an important thinker so deter appreciation of his efforts as Comte did through his discursive long-windedness, particularly in Positive Polity. The readings from his works below seek to exemplify his ideas while avoiding the torrent of words with which he surrounded them.

1. Aristotle, Montesquieu, Condorcet, Adam Smith, Bossuet

The name of Aristotle first presents itself, his memorable Politics being one of the finest productions of antiquity, and furnishing the general type of most of the works on that subject that have followed. This treatise could not possibly disclose any sense of the progressive tendencies of humanity, nor the slightest glimpse of the national laws of civilization; and it was necessarily occupied by metaphysical discussions of the principle and form of government: but it is truly marvellous that any mind should have produced a work so advanced, and even nearer to a positive view than his other works, at a time when political observation was restricted to a uniform and preliminary social state, and when the nascent positive spirit lived feebly in geometry alone. The analysis by which he refuted the dangerous fancies of Plato and his imitators about community of property evidences a rectitude, a sagacity, and a strength, which, in their application to such subjects, have been rarely equalled, and never surpassed. . . .

The first and most important series of works which then presents itself is that of Montesquieu, first, in his treatise on the Greatness and Decline of the Romans, and afterward in his Spirit of Laws. The

SOURCE: Positive Philosophy, pp. 442–44, 446–47, 449–50.

great strength of this memorable work appears to me to lie in its tendency to regard political phenomena as subject to invariable laws, like all other phenomena. This is manifested at the very outset, in the preliminary chapter, in which, for the first time in the history of the human mind, the general idea of *law* is directly defined, in relation to all, even to political subjects, in the same sense in which it is applied in the simplest positive investigations. The progress of science which had been effected by the labors of Descartes, Galileo, and Kepler, a century before, had rendered the most advanced minds familiar with an incomplete notion of progress. Montesquieu's conception was a generalization of this incomplete notion: and, instead of denying originality to so eminent a service, we may well be amazed that such a conception should be offered, before the positive method had extended beyond the simplest natural phenomena,—being scarcely admitted into the department of chemistry, and not yet heard of in the study of living bodies. And, in the other view, a man must have been in advance of his time, who could conceive of natural laws as the basis of social speculation and action, while all other able men were talking about the absolute and indefinite power of legislators, when armed with due authority, to modify at will the social state. The very qualities, however, which give its pre-eminence to Montesquieu's work prove to us the impossibility of success in an enterprise so premature in regard to its proposed object, the very conditions of which were still impracticable. The project of the work is not fulfilled in its course; and, admirable as are some of its details, it falls back, like all others, upon the primitive type offered by Aristotle's treatise. We find no reference of social phenomena to the laws whose existence was announced at the outset; nor any scientific selection and connection of facts. The general nature of his practical conclusions seems to show how far the execution of his work was from corresponding with his original intention; for his desultory review of the whole mass of social subjects ends in his setting up, as a universal political type, the English parliamentary system, the insufficiency of which, for the satisfaction of modern social requirements, was not, it is true, so conspicuous in his day as it is now, but still discernible enough, as we shall have occasion to see. It was honorable to Montesquieu's philosophical character, that he steered wide of the metaphysical Utopias which lay in his way, and resorted rather to the narrow anchorage at which he rested; but such a resort, so narrow and so barren, proves that he had wandered away from the course announced by himself. The only part of the book which bears any true marks of sustained positivity is that in which the social influence of permanent local causes—of that which, in political language, we may call climate—is considered. This view, evidently derived from Hippocrates, manifests a tendency to attach observed phenomena to forces able to produce them, as in natural philosophy; but the aim has failed. The true political influence of climate is misconceived, and usually much exaggerated, through the common error of analyzing a mere modification before the main action is fully understood; which is much like trying to determine planetary perturbations before ascertaining the chief gravitations. This error was inevitable under Montesquieu's necessary ignorance of the great social laws, while he was bent upon introducing the positive spirit into the domain of politics. He naturally betook himself to the only class of social speculations which seemed fit for his purpose. Pardonable or unavoidable as was his failure, it is a new evidence of the vast gap which lies open at the outset of the science. Montesquieu did not even perceive, any more than others, the fact which should regulate the whole political theory of climate; —that local physical causes, very powerful in the early days of civilization, lose their force in proportion as human development admits of their being neutralized: a view which would certainly have occurred to Montesquieu if he had possessed himself of the fundamental notion of human progression before he treated of the political theory of climate. Thus, this great philosopher proposed a grand enterprise which was premature in two senses, and in which he could not but fail,—first, by bringing social phenomena under the operation of the positive spirit before it had been introduced into the system of biological science; and again, in proposing social reorganization during a period marked out for revolutionary action. This explains why a mind so eminent should have exercised, through its very advancement, an immediate influence very inferior to that of a mere sophist, like Rousseau, whose intellectual state, much better adapted to the disposition of his contemporaries, allowed him to constitute himself, with so remarkable a success, the natural organ of the revolutionary movement of the time. It is by our posterity that Montesquieu will be duly estimated, when the extension of the positive philosophy to social speculations will disclose the high value of the precocious attempts which, though doomed to failure, yield the light by which the general question must be laid down.

After Montesquieu, the next great addition to Sociology (which is the term I may be allowed to invent to designate Social Physics) was made by Condorcet, proceeding on the views suggested by his illustrious friend Turgot. Turgot's suggestions with regard to the theory of the perfectability of human nature were doubtless the basis of Condorcet's speculation exhibited in his Historical Sketch of the Progress of the Human Mind, in which the scientific conception of the social progression of the race was, for the first time, clearly and directly proposed, with a distinct assertion of its primary importance. . . .

We can not impute to political economists any design to establish social science; for it is the express assertion of the most classical among them that their subject is wholly distinct from, and independent of general political science. Yet, sincere as they doubtless are in their dogma of isolation, they are no less sincerely persuaded that they have applied the positive spirit to economical science; and they perpetually set forth their method as the type by which all social theories will be finally regenerated. As this pretension has obtained credit enough to procure the establishment of several professorships for this species of instruction, I find myself obliged to explain why it is that I can not, as would be very desirable, propose to carry on my enterprise from the point reached by these philosophers, but must begin from the beginning. My criticism on political economy in this place is merely for the purpose of showing that it is not the philosophical creation that we want; and I must refer to my exposition as a whole any objectors to my summary estimate of political economy.

It is unfavorable to the philosophical pretensions of the economists that, being almost invariably lawyers or literary men, they have had no opportunity of discipline in that spirit of positive rationality which they suppose they have introduced into their researches. Precluded by their education from any idea of scientific observation of even the smallest phenomena, from any notion of natural laws, from all perception of what demonstration is, they must obviously be incapable of applying, impromptu, a method in which they have had no practice to the most difficult of all analyses. The only philosophical preparation that they can show is a set of vague precepts of general logic, susceptible of no real use; and thus, their conceptions present a purely metaphysical character. There is one great exceptional case which I must at once exempt from this criticism—that of the illustrious philosopher, Adam Smith, who made no pretension to found a new special science, but merely proposed (what he admirably achieved) to illustrate some leading points of social philosophy by luminous analyses relating to the division of employments, the function of money, the general action of banks, etc., and other chief portions of the industrial developments of the human race. Though involved, like all his contemporaries, in the metaphysical philosophy, a mind of such quality as his could not, however distinguished in the metaphysical school, be blinded by its illusions, because his preparatory studies had impressed him with a sense of what constitutes a true scientific method, as is clearly proved by the valuable sketches of the philosophical history of the sciences, and of astronomy in particular, which are published among his posthumous works. . . .

The temporary predilection of men's minds for political economy is, in truth, a new and strong illustration of the instinctive need which prevails to subject social researches to positive methods; and if that were once done, the interest in political economy would disappear. Various other signs of the times testify to the same disposition, which indeed pervades the whole action of our intelligences. I will refer to only one among the multitude of those signs; but it is one which aids in bringing about the satisfaction of the need. I mean the growing inclination for historical study, and the great improvement in that kind of research within two centuries.

Bossuet was, unquestionably, the first who proposed to survey, from a lofty point of view, the whole of the past of society. We can not adopt his explanations, easily derived from theological resources; but the spirit of universality, so thoroughly appreciated, and, under the circumstances, so wonderfully sustained, will always preserve this admirable composition* as a model, suggesting the true result of historical analysis;—the rational co-ordination of the great series of human events, according to a single design; which must, however, be more genuine and complete than that of Bossuet. There is no doubt that this fine piece of instruction has contributed, during both the past and the present century, to the improvement in the character of the chief historical compositions, especially in France and England, and afterward in Germany. Still, history has more of a literary and descriptive than of a scientific character. It does not yet establish a rational filiation in the series of social events, so as to admit (as in other sciences, and allowing for its greater complexity) of any degree of systematic prevision of their future succession. Perhaps the imputation of rashness cast upon the mere proposal of such a treatment of history is the

* *Discourse on Natural History.*

strongest confirmation we could have of its present unscientific character; for such prevision is everywhere else admitted to be the ultimate scientific test. Another evidence exists in the easy credit daily obtained by misty historical theories which explain nothing, and which testify to the literary and metaphysical bias under which history is studied, by minds unacquainted with the great scientific movement of modern times. Again, another evidence is the dogmatic separation which it is attempted to keep up between history and politics. Still, we must admit the growing taste of our age for historical labors to be a happy symptom of philosophical regeneration, however the inclination may be wasted upon superficial and misleading works, sometimes written with a view to immediate popularity by ministering to the popular taste. One of the most promising incidents of the time is the introduction into the highly metaphysical class of jurists of an historical school which has undertaken to connect, during every period of history, the whole of its legislation with the corresponding state of society. . . .

Attempts to constitute a science of society would not have been so obstinate, nor pursued in ways so various, if an instinctive need of it had not been deeply felt. At the same time, the general analysis of the chief efforts hitherto made explains their failure, and convinces us that the whole enterprise remains to be even conceived of in a manner which will secure its accomplishment. Nothing now prevents our going on to the fulfillment of this proposed task, by entering . . . on the study of the method in Social Physics. We have so ascertained and cleared our ground . . . that we are at full liberty to follow the speculative development . . . which will close with the co-ordination between the theory and practice of Social Physics.

2. The French Revolution

What was required . . . for the discovery of Sociological laws, and for the establishment upon these laws of a sound philosophical system, was an intellect in the vigour of youth, imbued with all the ardour of the revolutionary spirit, and yet spontaneously assimilating all that was valuable in the attempts of the retrograde school to appreciate the historical importance of the Middle Ages. In this

SOURCE: *Positive Polity*, Vol. I, pp. 50–56.

way and in no other could the true spirit of history arise. For that spirit consists in the sense of human continuity, which had hitherto been felt by no one, not even by my illustrious and unfortunate predecessor Condorcet. Meantime the genius of Gall was completing the recent attempts to systematize biology, by commencing the study of the internal functions of the brain; as far at least as these could be understood from the phenomena of individual as distinct from social development. This completes the series of social and intellectual conditions by which the discovery of sociological laws, and consequently the foundation of Positivism, was fixed for the precise date at which I began my philosophical career: that is to say, one generation after the progressive dictatorship of the Convention, and almost immediately after the fall of the retrograde tyranny of Bonaparte.

Thus it appears that the revolutionary movement, and the long period of reaction which succeeded it, were alike necessary, before the new general doctrine could be distinctly conceived of as a whole. And if this preparation was needed for the establishment of Positivism as a philosophical system, far more needful was it for the recognition of its social value. For it guaranteed free exposition and discussion of opinion: and it led the public to look to Positivism as the system which contained in germ the ultimate solution of social problems. . . .

Having satisfied ourselves of the dependence of Positivism upon the first phase of the Revolution, we have now to consider it as the future guide of the second phase.

It is often supposed that the destruction of the old regime was brought about by the Revolution. But history when carefully examined points to a very different conclusion. It shows that the Revolution was not the cause but the consequence of the utter decomposition of the mediæval system; a process which had been going on for five centuries throughout Western Europe, and especially in France; spontaneously at first, and afterwards in a more systematic way. The Revolution, far from protracting the negative movement of previous centuries, was a bar to its further extension. It was a final outbreak in which men showed their irrevocable purpose of abandoning the old system altogether, and of proceeding at once to the task of entire reconstruction. The most conclusive proof of this intention was given by the abolition of royalty; which had been the rallying point of all the decaying remnants of the old French constitution. . . .

The first period of the Revolution produced results of an extremely negative and destructive kind. In fact the movement was in this respect a failure. This is partly to be attributed to the pressing necessities of the hard struggle for national independence which France maintained so gloriously against the combined attacks of the retrograde nations of Europe. But it is far more largely owing to the purely critical character of the metaphysical doctrines by which the revolutionary spirit was at that time directed. . . .

The doctrine by which social regeneration is now to be directed, could not have arisen previously to the Revolution. The impulse which the Revolution gave to thought was indispensable to its formation. Here then was an insurmountable fatality by which men were forced to make use of the critical principles which had been found serviceable in former struggles, as the only available instruments for construction. As soon as the old order had once been fairly abandoned, there was of course no utility whatever in the negative philosophy. But its doctrines had become familiar to men's minds, and its motto of 'Liberty and Equality,' was at that time the one most compatible with social progress. Thus the first stage of the revolutionary movement was accomplished under the influence of principles that had become obsolete, and that were quite inadequate to the new task required of them. . . . The incapacity for construction of the doctrine in which the revolutionary spirit had embodied itself was placed beyond the reach of doubt. The result was to impress everyone with the deep urgent necessity for social renovation; but the principles of that renovation were still left undetermined.

In this condition of philosophical and political opinion, the necessity of Order was felt to be paramount, and a long period of reaction ensued. . . . The only permanent result of this period was the historical and doctrinal evidence brought forward by De Maistre and his school, of the social inutility of modern metaphysics, while at the same time their intellectual weakness was being proved by the successful attempts of Cabanis, and still more of Gall, to extend the Positive method to the highest biological questions. In all other respects this elaborate attempt to prevent the final emancipation of Humanity proved a complete failure; in fact, it led to a revival of the instinct of Progress. . . .

A re-awakening of the revolutionary spirit was then inevitable; and it took place as soon as peace was established, and the chief support of the retrograde system had been thus removed. The doctrines of negation were called back to life; but very little illusion

now remained as to their capacity for organising. In want of something better, men accepted them as a means of resisting retrograde
principles, just as these last had owed their apparent success to
the necessity of checking the tendency to anarchy. Amidst these fresh
debates on worn-out subjects, the public soon became aware that
a final solution of the question had not yet arisen even in germ. It
therefore concerned itself for little except the maintenance of Order
and Liberty; conditions as indispensable for the free action of philosophy as for material prosperity. The whole position was most
favourable for the construction of a definite solution; and it was, in
fact, during the last phase of the retrograde movement that the
elementary principle of a solution was furnished, by my discovery in
1822 of the two-fold law of intellectual development.

The apparent indifference of the public, to whom all the existing
parties seemed equally devoid of insight into the political future,
was at last mistaken by a blind government for tacit consent to its
unwise schemes. The cause of Progress was in danger. Then came
the memorable crisis of 1830, by which the system of reaction,
introduced thirty-six years previously, was brought to an end. The
convictions which that system inspired were indeed so superficial,
that its supporters came of their own accord to disavow them, and
uphold in their own fashion the chief revolutionary doctrines. These
again were abandoned by their previous supporters on their accession
to power. When the history of these times is written, nothing
will give a clearer view of the revulsion of feeling on both sides
than the debates which took place on Liberty of Education. . . .
All the opinions of the day had become alike utterly incompatible,
both with Order and with Progress. The Conservative school
undertook to reconcile the two; but it had no constructive power;
and the only result of its doctrines was to give equal encouragement
to anarchy and to reaction, so as to be able always to neutralise
the one by the other. The establishment of Constitutional Monarchy was now put forward as the ultimate issue of the great Revolution. But no one could seriously place any real confidence in a
system so alien to the whole character of French history, offering
as it did nothing but a superficial and unwise imitation of a political
anomaly essentially peculiar to England.

The period then between 1830 and 1848 may be regarded as
a natural pause in the political movement. The reaction which
succeeded the original crisis had exhausted itself; but the final
or organic phase of the Revolution was still delayed for want of

definite principles to guide it. No conception had been formed of it, except by a small number of philosophic minds who had taken their stand upon the recently established laws of social science, and had found themselves able, without recourse to any chimerical views, to gain some general insight into the political future, of which Condorcet, my principal predecessor, knew so little. But it was impossible for the regenerating doctrine to spread more widely and to be accepted as the peaceful solution of social problems, until a distinct refutation had been given of the false assertion so authoritatively made that the parliamentary system was the ultimate issue of the Revolution. This notion once destroyed, the work of spiritual reorganisation should be left entirely to the free efforts of independent thinkers. . . .

Viewed negatively, the principle of Republicanism sums up the first phase of the Revolution. It precludes the possibility of recurrence to Royalism, which, ever since the second half of the reign of Louis XIV., has been the rallying point of all reactionist tendencies. Interpreting the principle in its positive sense, we may regard it as a direct step towards the final regeneration of society. By consecrating all human forces of whatever kind to the general service of the community, Republicanism recognises the doctrine of subordinating Politics to Morals. . . . The direct tendency, then, of the French Republic is to sanction the fundamental principle of Positivism, the preponderance, namely, of Feeling over Intellect and Activity. Starting from this point, public opinion will soon be convinced that the work of organising society on republican principles is one which can only be performed by the new philosophy. . . .

3. Resolution of Social Anarchy

The decline of the theological philosophy and the corresponding spiritual power has left society without any moral discipline. Hence a series of effects which I shall mark in the order of their natural connection . . . 1. A complete mental dispersion . . . 2. The almost total absence of public morality . . . 3. The social preponderance which during the last three centuries has been, more and more, assigned to the purely material point of view, is another manifest

SOURCE: *Positive Polity*, Vol. IV (1826 essay), pp. 623–26.

result of the spiritual disorganization of modern nations . . . 4. I must point out, as the last general consequence of the dissolution of the spiritual power, the establishment of that modern autocracy without parallel in history, and which, for want of a more adequate expression, may be styled ministerialism or administrative despotism. Its peculiar organic character is the centralization of power, pushed further and further, beyond all reasonable bounds, and its usual mode of action is systematic corruption. Both inevitably result from the moral disorganization of society. . . .

3

Law of the Three Stages or States

The terms "states" and "stages" have been used interchangeably by commentators and translators and both are acceptable as terms in Comte's fundamental law provided we know what they stand for. Yet there would be less ambiguity if all were to use the term "states," for what Comte means in this connection are "states of mind"—the states through which the human intellect passes on its way to the scientific or positivist. Such understanding of his meaning is indispensable to an appreciation of his famous "law." Otherwise, his entire system of thought can be misconstrued as materialistic, whereas in the fundamental and final analysis it is unalterably intellectual, that is, philosophical. "Mind" is for Comte the fundamental philosophical and, hence, the fundamental sociological concept.

By the theological state, Comte meant the general philosophical climate in which natural phenomena (that is, phenomena which later become scientific data) are interpreted supernaturally. They are explained through concocted mythologies as the work of fantastic beings. In short, the "theological" involves divinities that are anthropomorphic—the gods do man's thinking for him. But by theological he does not mean religious. Man never ceases to be religious—never ceases to have faith—even in the positivistic state.

By the metaphysical state, Comte means turning to empty abstractions as explanation of phenomena; for example, disembodied Nature, or élan vital (vital force) in Henri Bergson's sense, or the concept of the soul in psychology. Metaphysical man thus finds the world comprehensible not through the unity underlying the philosophy of science but through seeking for final causes and substituting Nature for God. Though the metaphysical is a transitional state bearing traces of theology's divorce from science, it advances beyond theology by seeking for natural laws and some consistency in scientific viewpoint. It reaches its apex, for Comte, in the critical philosophy of the Enlightenment represented by the French Deists, the French Encyclopedists, and the German idealist philosopher, Immanuel Kant. But even with them it still bears a theological tinge; the metaphysical stage is, so to speak, the sunset of theologism and the sunrise of positivism. Metaphysical thinking is in continual change and upheaval; it contains its own sources of intellectual dissatisfaction. Ultimately, it becomes unsystematic in relation to the interpretation of the sciences and dissolves into endless logomachy.

Positivism arises not from the individual mind contemplating itself like some introspective Faust in his study but from seeing the individual as representing humanity. Thus, individual man becomes the object of science (sociology) as the epitome of humanity and he also becomes the subject making science possible—the affectual organism pursuing the path of truth. *Reasoning + observation*

The early explanation of the law of three stages or states was made by Comte in an essay in 1825. The excerpt below is the more mature statement from the Cours. *The law of the three stages outlines the intellectual stations thro which the human mind passes on its way to forging a science.*

1. The Fundamental Law

In the theological state, the human mind, seeking the essential nature of beings, the first and final causes (the origin and purpose) of all effects—in short, Absolute knowledge—supposes all phenomena to be produced by the immediate action of supernatural beings.

In the metaphysical state, which is only a modification of the first, the mind supposes, instead of supernatural beings, abstract forces, veritable entities (that is, personified abstractions) inherent in all beings, and capable of producing all phenomena. What is called the explanation of phenomena is, in this stage, a mere reference of each to its proper entity.

In the final, the positive state, the mind has given over the vain search after Absolute notions, the origin and destination of the universe, and the causes of phenomena, and applies itself to the study of their laws—that is, their invariable relations of succession and resemblance. Reasoning and observation, duly combined, are

SOURCE: *Positive Philosophy*, pp. 26–28.

the means of this knowledge. What is now understood when we speak of an explanation of facts is simply the establishment of a connection between single phenomena and some general facts, the number of which continually diminishes with the progress of science.

The Theological system arrived at the highest perfection of which it is capable when it substituted the providential action of a single Being for the varied operations of the numerous divinities which had been before imagined. In the same way, in the last stage of the Metaphysical system, men substitute one great entity (Nature) as the cause of all phenomena, instead of the multitude of entities at first supposed. In the same way, again, the ultimate perfection of the Positive system would be (if such perfection could be hoped for) to represent all phenomena as particular aspects of a single general fact—such as Gravitation, for instance.

The importance of the working of this general law will be established hereafter. At present, it must suffice to point out some of the grounds of it.

There is no science which, having attained the positive stage, does not bear marks of having passed through the others. Some time since, it was (whatever it might be) composed, as we can now perceive, of metaphysical abstractions; and, further back in the course of time, it took its form from theological conceptions. We shall have only too much occasion to see . . . that our most advanced sciences still bear very evident marks of the two earlier periods through which they have passed.

The progress of the individual mind is not only an illustration, but an indirect evidence of that of the general mind. The point of departure of the individual and of the race being the same, the phases of the mind of a man correspond to the epochs of the mind of the race. Now, each of us is aware, if he looks back upon his own history, that he was a theologian in his childhood, a metaphysician in his youth, and a natural philosopher in his manhood. All men who are up to their age can verify this for themselves.

Besides the observation of facts, we have theoretical reasons in support of this law.

The most important of these reasons arises from the necessity that always exists for some theory to which to refer our facts, combined with the clear impossibility that, at the outset of human knowledge, men could have formed theories out of the observation of facts. All good intellects have repeated, since Bacon's time, that there can be no real knowledge but that which is based on observed facts. This is incontestable, in our present advanced stage; but, if we look back to the primitive stage of human knowledge, we shall see that it must have been otherwise then. If it is true that every theory must be based upon observed facts, it is equally true that facts can not be observed without the guidance of some theory. Without such guidance, our facts would be desultory and fruitless; we could not retain them: for the most part we could not even perceive them.

Thus, between the necessity of observing facts in order to form a theory, and having a theory in order to observe facts, the human mind would have been entangled in a vicious circle, but for the natural opening afforded by Theological conceptions. This is the fundamental reason for the theological character of the primitive philosophy. This necessity is confirmed by the perfect suitability of the theological philosophy to the earliest researches of the human mind. It is remarkable that the most inaccessible questions —those of the nature of beings, and the origin and purpose of phenomena—should be the first to occur in a primitive state, while those which are really within our reach are regarded as almost unworthy of serious study. The reason is evident enough:—that experience alone can teach us the measure of our powers; and if men had not begun by an exaggerated estimate of what they can do, they would never have done all that they are capable of. Our organization requires this. At such a period there could have been no reception of a positive philosophy, whose function is to discover the laws of phenomena, and whose leading characteristic it is to regard as interdicted to human reason those sublime mysteries which theology explains, even to their minutest details, with the most attractive facility. It is just so under a practical view of the nature of the researches with which men first occupied themselves. Such inquiries offered the powerful charm of unlimited empire over the external world—a world destined wholly for our use, and involved in every way with our existence. The theological philosophy, presenting this view, administered exactly the stimulus necessary to incite the human mind to the irksome labor without which it could make no progress. We can now scarcely conceive of such a state of things, our reason having become sufficiently mature to enter upon laborious scientific researches, without needing any such stimulus as wrought upon the imaginations of astrologers and alchemists. We have motive enough in the hope of discovering the laws of phenomena, with a view to the confirmation or rejection of a theory. But it could not be so in the earliest days; and it is to the chimeras of astrology and alchemy that we owe the long series of observations and experiments on which our positive science is based. Kepler felt this on behalf of astronomy, and Berthollet on behalf of chemistry. Thus was a spontaneous philosophy, the theological, the only possible beginning, method, and provisional system, out of which the Positive philosophy could grow. It is easy, after this, to perceive how Metaphysical methods and doctrines must have afforded the means of transition from the one to the other.

The human understanding, slow in its advance, could not step at once from the theological into the positive philosophy. The two are so radically opposed, that an intermediate system of conceptions has been necessary to render the transition possible. It is only in doing this, that metaphysical conceptions have any utility whatever. In contemplating phenomena, men substitute for supernatural direction a corresponding entity. This entity may have been supposed to be derived from the supernatural action: but it is more easily lost sight of, leaving attention free from the facts themselves, till, at length, metaphysical agents have ceased to be anything more than the abstract names of phenomena. It is not easy to say by what other process than this our minds could have passed from supernatural considerations to natural; from the theological system to the positive.

4

The Meaning and Advantages of "Positivism"

Before the positivist approach to social phenomena, systematic consideration of human relationships aimed either to defend their existing status, to speculate on utopia, or to seek to reorganize those relationships without knowledge of laws explaining them. Comte considers that positivism for the first time makes possible the systematic understanding of the laws connecting and comprehending social phenomena as the basis for general social reorganization. Lack of social laws leads to inadequacy of social reorganization. This scientific understanding (as distinct from mere erudition or resort to authority or untamed speculation) was not possible until the sciences of the inorganic and organic worlds had reached some definitive stage. That stage was finally achieved in the nineteenth century as the theologico-metaphysical doctrines underlying these sciences collapsed. It then became possible to bring social phenomena into the ambit of positivity.

The terms "positive" and "positivism" are not highly felicitous, certainly not in English. They sound as if journey's end had been reached in the search for validated knowledge. But this view is completely erroneous. Positivism is a state of mind—the scientific state of mind seeking laws of the behavior of phenomena in place of the vain search for causes in the theologico-metaphysical states. It aims to validate hypotheses by resort to facts; it aims to predict future occurrences on the basis of analyses of past uniformities of relationships; it aims to discover the laws of statics or coexistences of regularities in the social organism and the laws of succession from scientific study of factors inducing change.

Indeed, Comte does not grow weary of emphasizing that positivism rests on relativism of conception and not on absolutism. All subject matters are relative in their validity to the historical epoch in which their laws are propounded.

The laws of logic can only be discovered by studying the history of the application of scientific method in the development and interdevelopment of the sciences from mathematics and astronomy to sociology. The sciences reveal a unity of intellectual approach, for their aim is the search for the general laws which underlie specific subject matters. Thus, the permanent revolution is the discovery of the homogeneity of intellectual processes by which man comes to comprehend (and thus becomes able to control) his universe. This discovery stems from the inextricable connection of the conditions of social existence with the development of intellect. Hence the laws of social behavior lead to the discovery that these variable conditions have determined the course of the sciences which have led up to them. What man arrives at last scientifically is what he has been looking for from the very beginning of his search for meaning. Sociology permits man to express what was always latent in him but held back by theologico-metaphysical barriers. In short, historical consciousness based on the laws of social dynamics will lead man to discover his future through self-understanding, a self-understanding which comes about through his ability to modify the world by basing his devices for social control upon the laws he has discovered.

Social progress does not arise from the pursuit of happiness but from developments in human beliefs and aspirations brought about by broadening the base of scientific understanding. Happiness comes from positivistic wisdom; the pursuit of happiness by itself is a canard.

Every historical epoch sets limits upon the changes possible. Yet these limits are broad enough to enlarge the scope of positivist understanding and the scope of action based upon such understanding. Man's free will is historical free will. He is determined in his actions by his understanding, at a given time, of science and not by subservience to either the gods of theology or the disembodied entities of metaphysics.

1. The Meaning of the Word "Positive"

On reviewing . . . the intellectual character of Positivism, it will be seen that all its essential attributes are summed up in the word *Positive*, which I applied to the new philosophy at its outset. All the languages of Western Europe agree in understanding by this word and its derivatives the two qualities of *reality* and *usefulness*. Combining these, we get at once an adequate definition of the true philosophic spirit, which, after all, is nothing but good sense generalised and put into a systematic form. The term also implies in all European languages, *certainty* and *precision*, qualities by which the intellect of modern nations is markedly distinguished from that of antiquity. Again, the ordinary acceptation of the term implies a directly *organic* tendency. Now the metaphysical spirit is incapable of organising; it can only criticise. This distinguishes it from the Positive spirit, although for a time they had a common sphere of action. By speaking of Positivism as organic, we imply that it has a social purpose; that purpose being to supersede Theology in the spiritual direction of the human race.

But the word will bear yet a further meaning. The organic character of the system leads us naturally to another of its attributes, namely, its invariable *relativity*. Modern thinkers will never rise above that critical position which they have hitherto taken up towards the past except by repudiating all absolute principles. This last meaning is more latent than the others, but is really contained in the term. It will soon become generally accepted, and the word *Positive* will be understood to mean *relative* as much as it now means organic, precise, certain, useful, and real. Thus the highest attributes of human wisdom have, with one exception, been gradually condensed into a single expressive term. All that is now wanting is that the word should denote what at first could form no part of the meaning, the union of moral with intellectual qualities. At present, only the latter are included; but the course of modern progress makes it certain that the conception implied by the word Positive will ultimately have a more direct reference to the heart than to the understanding. For it will soon be felt by all that the tendency of Positivism, and that by virtue of its primary characteristic, reality,

SOURCE: *Positive Polity*, Vol. I, pp. 44–45.

is to make Feeling systematically supreme over Reason as well as over Activity. After all, the change consists simply in realising the full etymological value of the word *Philosophy*. For it was impossible to realise it until moral and mental conditions had been reconciled; and this has been now done by the foundation of a Positive science of society.

2. *Character and Advantages of the Positive Philosophy*

. . . The first characteristic of the Positive Philosophy is that it regards all phenomena as subjected to invariable natural *Laws*. . . .

II. The second effect of the Positive Philosophy, an effect not less important and far more urgently wanted, will be to regenerate Education. . . .

III. The same special study of scientific generalities must also aid the progress of the respective positive sciences: and this constitutes our third head of advantages. . . .

IV. The Positive Philosophy offers the only solid basis for that Social Reorganization which must succeed the critical condition in which the most civilized nations are now living. . . .

Leaving these four points of advantage, we must attend to one precautionary reflection.

Because it is proposed to consolidate the whole of our acquired knowledge into one body of homogeneous doctrine, it must not be supposed that we are going to study this vast variety as proceeding from a single principle, and as subjected to a single law. There is something so chimerical in attempts at universal explanation by a single law, that it may be as well to secure this Work at once from an imputation of the kind, though its development will show how undeserved such an imputation would be. Our intellectual resources are too narrow, and the universe is too complex, to leave any hope that it will ever be within our power to carry scientific perfection to its last degree of simplicity. Moreover, it appears as if the value of such an attainment, supposing it possible, were greatly overrated. . . . The consideration of all phenomena as referable to a single origin is by no means necessary to the systematic formation of

SOURCE: *Positive Philosophy*, pp. 28, 34, 35, 36, 37–38.

science, any more than to the realization of the great and happy consequences that we anticipate from the positive philosophy. The only necessary unity is that of Method, which is already in great part established. As for the doctrine, it need not be one; it is enough that it be homogeneous. . . . While pursuing the philosophical aim of all science, the lessening of the number of general laws requisite for the explanation of natural phenomena, we shall regard as presumptuous every attempt, in all future time, to reduce them rigorously to one.

3. Positive Method in Relation to Social Phenomena

If we contemplate the positive spirit in its relation to scientific conception . . . we shall find that this philosophy is distinguished from the theologico-metaphysical by its tendency to render relative the ideas which were at first absolute. This inevitable passage from the absolute to the relative is one of the most important philosophical results of each of the intellectual revolutions which has carried on every kind of speculation from the theological or metaphysical to the scientific state. In a scientific view, this contrast between the relative and the absolute may be regarded as the most decisive manifestation of the antipathy between the modern philosophy and the ancient.

. . . Now, it is obvious that the absolute spirit characterizes social speculation now, wherever it exists, as the different schools are all agreed in looking for an immutable political type, which makes no allowance for the regular modification of political conceptions according to the variable state of civilization. This absolute spirit, having prevailed through all social changes, and their corresponding philosophical divergences, is now so inherent in existing political science that it affords, amid all its enormous evils, the only means of restraining individual eccentricities, and excluding the influx of arbitrarily variable opinions. . . .

There is no change of order and agreement but in subjecting social phenomena, like all others, to invariable natural laws, which shall, as a whole, prescribe for each period, with entire certainty, the

SOURCE: *Positive Philosophy*, pp. 453, 455, 467–68.

limits and character of political action—in other words, introducing into the study of social phenomena the same positive spirit which has regenerated every other branch of human speculation. Such a procedure is the true scientific basis of human dignity; as the chief tendencies of man's nature thus acquire a solemn character of authority which must be always respected by rational legislation; whereas the existing belief in the indefinite power of political combinations, which seems at first to exalt the importance of Man, issues in attributing to him a sort of social automatism passively directed by some supremacy of either Providence or the human ruler. . . .

We have nothing to do here with the metaphysical controversy about the absolute happiness of Man at different stages of civilization. As the happiness of every man depends on the harmony between the development of his various faculties and the entire system of the circumstances which govern his life; and as, on the other hand, this equilibrium always establishes itself spontaneously to a certain extent, it is impossible to compare in a positive way, either by sentiment or reasoning, the individual welfare which belongs to social situations that can never be brought into direct comparison. . . . To me it appears that the amelioration is as unquestionable as the development from which it proceeds, provided we regard it as subject, like the development itself, to limits, general and special, which science will be found to prescribe. The chimerical notion of unlimited perfectibility is thus at once excluded. Taking the human race as a whole, and not any one people, it appears that human development brings after it, in two ways, an ever-growing amelioration, first, in the radical condition of Man, which no one disputes: and next, in his corresponding faculties, which is a view much less attended to. There is no need to dwell upon the improvement in the conditions of human existence, both by the increasing action of Man on his environment through the advancement of the sciences and arts, and by the constant amelioration of his customs and manners; and again, by the gradual improvement in social organization. . . . The tendency to improvement must be highly spontaneous and irresistible to have persevered notwithstanding the enormous faults—political faults especially—which have at all times absorbed or neutralized the greater part of our social forces. Even throughout the revolutionary period, in spite of the marked discordance between the political system and the general state of civilization, the improvement has proceeded, not only in physical and intellectual, but also in moral respects, though the transient disorganization could not but disturb the natural evolution. As for the other aspect of the question, the gradual and slow improvement of human nature, within narrow limits, it seems to me impossible to reject altogether the principle proposed (with great exaggeration, however) by Lamarck, of the necessary influence of a homogeneous and continuous exercise in producing, in every animal organism, and especially in Man, an organic improvement, susceptible of being established in the race, after a sufficient persistence. If we take the best-marked case—that of intellectual development, it seems to be unquestionable that there is a superior aptitude for mental combinations, independent of all culture, among highly-civilized people; or, what comes to the same thing, an inferior aptitude among nations that are less advanced—the average intellect of the members of those societies being taken for observation. The intellectual faculties are, it is true, more modified than the others by the social evolution; but then they have the smallest relative effect in the individual human constitution: so that we are authorized to infer from their amelioration a proportionate improvement in aptitudes that are more marked and equally exercised. In regard to morals, particularly, I think it indisputable that the gradual development of humanity favors a growing preponderance of the noblest tendencies of our nature. . . . These two aspects of social evolution, then,—the *development* which brings after it the *improvement*, we may consider to be admitted as facts. . . .

5

Some Commentary on Comte's
View of Man's Logic
and the Sciences

In his book Reconstruction in Philosophy, John Dewey wrote that philosophy must cease to deal with the problems of philosophers and begin to deal with the problems of men. Along this same line of reasoning, almost a hundred years before, Comte realized that what seem like the mundane problems of ordinary men often mask true philosophical problems. Their solution, however, must be sought through the sciences appropriate to each level of problems. Men should resort to science to solve the same problems which were formerly being answered through non-science (theology or metaphysics).

Once a science has begun to make headway it is taken up by more and more people. But every man cannot be a scientist and certainly not a universal mind. Instead, men learn slowly that scientific faith is the faith to abide by. For this faith to become general everyone must be exposed to an education which teaches science as an active, living system that deals with the problems men first couched in terms of so-called common sense. The task for education thus becomes awesome, and we are still far from having even approximated its demands.

It is astonishing that a group of over-zealous philosophers of science in the late nineteenth and early twentieth centuries should have claimed the right to take over Comte's term "positivism" and call their way of thinking "neo-positivism." All that they have in common with Comte is opposition to theology and metaphysics.

Scientific thinking unifies the mind but it does so not through absolutism but through understanding that scientific truth is in continual evolution and that it is relative—relative to the tentative character of scientific laws, to the development of technical instruments, to the shortcomings of our perceptual apparatus as human beings, and to the general climate of opinion.

Reductionism (a standpoint held by some neo-positivists) is a system in which phenomena of a higher level are explained in terms of phenomena of a lower level. Thus, on the reductionist thesis, biological phenomena are explained physio-chemically, economic phenomena mathematically, and the like. Comte considers reductionism a form of utopian nonsense. The methods of analysis and explanation for every science are determined by the type of phenomena with which it deals. As phenomena increase in complexity, for example in higher organic life, they become less and less capable of definitive explanation. Yet at the same time, their very complexity brings them closer to man's intervention in their operations since their complexity rests on their being human problems. It is the phenomena we have most difficulty in explaining that we can do most about.

On what later came to be known as the heredity-environment controversy, and certainly in regard to human nature, Comte took a position far in advance of his time. He arrived at the conclusion that the underlying emotional facets of man are universally the same but that the external environment (the "milieu," as he called it), both physical and historical, made adaptation indispensable. Though man is always in the process of "becoming," he cannot surpass the elements of his "being."

To understand the phenomena of the "higher sciences"—biology, psychology, sociology—we must come to realize that their data were not preordained for our comprehension. Indeed, they seem preordained, rather, to continually escape the exact knowledge we would like. God did not make the world for man's understanding; man originally made God in order to make the world seem comprehensible.

Regarding the problem of the character of scientific laws, Comte reaches an important distinction between the laws of the individual sciences and the few more general—the encyclopedic—laws of a unified philosophy of nature, man, and society. When Comte comes to the problem of the science of logic—the subject dealing with the laws of human thought—he criticizes the formal logicians in much the same way that John Locke criticized Aristotle, saying that Aristotle seemed to think that God first invented formal logic and then taught men how to think. To Comte, the laws of human thought can be discovered only through investigation of how men have developed their thinking processes and refined them through scientific investigations. Formal logic developed with man's mind and man's mind developed through use in science. Each science encourages new ways of thinking and methods of investigation. Men do not find method made for them; they struggle to achieve it. It is extremely doubtful that Comte would be sympathetic to the application of contemporary symbolic or mathematical logic in all the sciences. Yet, a sociologist must be trained in the methods of the other sciences, for in them he will see logic in use and the relation of a specific logic to a specific science.

For sociology to fulfill its task of giving men a faith to live by, it must become not merely one science among many but a philosophy for conducting life. This philosophy arises from the most fundamental of all laws—that science seeks to enlighten man concerning his own behavior. When positivism becomes universal all sciences become humanistic. This generalized humanism metamorphoses the intellect from an entity in itself into an instrument for affection. Enlightened emotion emerges as the keystone in the mosaic of science and all science is thus unified by its subservience to humanity.

Excellent discussions of Comte on the meaning of "science," "scientific phenomena and scientific laws," and "positive logic" can be found in Lévy-Bruhl's The Philosophy of Auguste Comte, pp. 61–78, 79–84, 86–91, 94–102, and 103–18.

6

Classification of the Sciences

It may appear that Comte's classification of the sciences is a cleverly contrived device for concealing pretensions to omniscience. But from the standpoints of both Comte's own enormous learning and the inexorable relationship of this classification to the law of the three states, this appearance is deceitful. Comte understood the material of the sciences so well that at the many lectures he delivered (which altogether became the Cours de philosophie positive), eminent scientists from the various disciplines attended, seeking to learn from him the philosophical presuppositions of their particular disciplines. With regard to the systematic ordering of Comte's world view, classification followed from the necessary sequence in which the sciences developed—according to the law of the three states. The classification is therefore, as he wrote, "the indispensable complement of the fundamental law" of the three states. One may go so far as to say that Comte's classification stands or falls with the validity of this fundamental law.

The hierarchy of the sciences is not concerned with each and every facet of science; rather it rests on classifying, in order of development (and over time in order of interdevelopment), the basic or abstract sciences from which subsidiary sciences flow. An abstract science is one which is ultimately not reducible in its principles—it is "fundamental."

Comte felt that the nineteenth century for the first time permitted a correct classification and that he was called upon to establish it. What an undertaking! It is little wonder that he was accused of hubris and unmitigated gall. But to the sadness of his antagonistic critics, he brought off the undertaking with magnificence.

The abstract sciences are mathematics, astronomy, physics, chemistry, biology (which he sometimes calls physiology), and sociology.

The order in which these sciences appear is not mechanical or completely chronological. They are arranged according to the state of their positivity (their law-making capacity). Or as Lévy-Bruhl wrote:

Comte does not mean to say that the fundamental sciences came into existence one after the other, nor that, for every one of them, each period is sufficiently explained by the period immediately preceding it. His thought is very different. On the contrary, he represents the development of the several sciences as simultaneous. They act and react one upon another in a thousand ways. Often some progress in a science is the direct effect of a discovery made in an art which has apparently no affinities with it. Such is, to quote an example which Comte could not in the least have foreseen, the progress of astronomical observations due to photography. In fact, the history of a science during a given period is closely allied to that of the other sciences and arts during the same time, or rather, to be more explicit, to the general history of civilisation. But their respective transitions to the positive state are accomplished in the order set forth in the classification. For individually they could not reach this state if the fundamental science preceding had not attained to it before them.

Herbert Spencer severely criticized Comte's classification by missing its main presuppositions. First, Spencer did not realize that Comte was establishing a hierarchy of abstract sciences. And second, and more important, Spencer saw Comte's establishment of two types of classification—objective and subjective—as a contradiction. But the subjectivity of the theological state is not the subjectivity of the positive state. The first is irrational subjectivity based upon supernatural intervention as the explanation of phenomena; the second is the subjectivity arising from the nature of man. When man becomes the object of positive science through psychology and sociology, we come to see the logical coherence of subject and object, since man is then both subject—scientist-observer—and the object of study. In short, sociology makes possible the scientific resuscitation of the subjective method as positive. Man becomes the center of the universe of science and thus the other sciences for the first time gain a positivistic unity.

Sociology, for Comte, not only crowns the hierarchy of the sciences but it also makes possible a sound philosophical basis for science in general. It shows the homogeneity of scientific method as socially determined and gives man a philosophy to live by. Contemporary sociology might well heed Comte's example by seeking to find a faith for man through its researches rather than continuing to be comprised of a body of disconnected researches held together by hindsight. The fields of sociology today are in such a state of dispersion as to make one wonder if the field of study Comte discovered has not been betrayed by compartmentalization, departmentalization, and academic bureaucratization.

Comte's discussion of the hierarchy of the positive sciences can be found in Positive Philosophy, pp. 38–50, and his distinction between objective and subjective methods of classification in Positive Polity, Vol. I, pp. 355–63.

7

Biology as Prolegomenal to Sociology

In addition to being the "father of sociology," Auguste Comte also helped bring into being and revolutionized the "philosophy of science," an accomplishment for which he has been given insufficient or no credit.

To Comte, the philosophy of science is not a compendium of methods common to all the individual sciences nor is it, as neo-positivists would have it, the expatiation of the blanket unity of science. Rather, it consists of the philosophical unity underlying all the sciences. That philosophy is positivism, which shows each science as an historically emergent sociological event. No science has a philosophy in and of itself; they are each part of man's universal search for meaning even when that search is directed toward non-human subject matter. The unity of the sciences stems from their humanistic orientation. The sciences—inorganic, organic, social—are human inventions amidst a hostile world; they must be wrung from it in a never-ending struggle whose conditions change as social relationships are transformed.

The sciences of life—biology, psychology, sociology—mark a break in the way phenomena are approached. They deal with dynamic phenomena subject to pathologies which themselves tell much about life. Once biology approaches a positivist state it necessarily carries with it sciences which will crown the hierarchy—psychology and sociology. With this climactic event, we discover that each science has really been part of the episodic and saltatory achievement of man. Each science has unwittingly brought a new vision of man that is not yet sociology but becomes fully understood sociologically once the great law of the three states opens the way to the final triumph

—man's discovery of himself as the standard by which the worth of science is to be judged. Thus, finally, he sees that without sociology further progress in any science is impossible and also that canons for his behavior, his customs, his laws, his institutions, and his politics can be appropriate to his historical period only on the basis of sociological laws. Through man sociology was discovered; through sociology the world in general is rediscovered.

1. Biology

The passage from the inorganic world to the world of Life constitutes a critical step in natural philosophy. Astronomy, Physics, and Chemistry represented successive steps in the same series. If each order of phenomena presented in itself something which was irreducible to previous orders, nevertheless all these phenomena, in a certain sense, remained homogeneous. Without rashness, Descartes could conceive that physics, like astronomy, would one day assume the mathematical form. And to-day more than one scientific man considers the distinction between physics and chemistry as provisional.

But as soon as life appears, we enter a new world. At this degree the "enrichment of the real" is suddenly so considerable that we find it difficult to admit the homogeneity of these phenomena with the preceding ones. Comte here reaps the benefit of his prudence. His philosophy has guarded against reducing all science to a single type, and it is content with the unity of method and the homogeneity of doctrine. It only demands that each science should limit itself to the search after the laws of phenomena. As to the way in which this research is to be carried out, it is evidently subordinated to the nature of the phenomena in question. Now, biological phenomena present a number of characteristics which belong to them alone, and the first duty of the positive science which studies them is to respect their originality. . . .

With biology, says Comte, necessarily appear the ideas of consensus, of hierarchy, of "milieu," of the conditions of existence, of the relation between the static and the dynamic states, between the organ and the function. In a word, a biological phenomenon, considered alone is devoid of meaning. Strictly speaking, it does not even

SOURCE: Lévy-Bruhl, *The Philosophy of Auguste Comte*, pp. 171–80, 185–87.

exist. It can only be understood by its relations with the other phenomena which take place in the living being, phenomena which react upon it. At the same time it reacts upon them. Here, in opposition to what takes place in the inorganic world, the parts are only intelligible through the idea of the whole. Undoubtedly a certain solidarity of phenomena exists in the inorganic world, which allows us to consider united wholes in it. But the solidarity of biological phenomena is far closer, for without it we could not conceive them, while, as regards the phenomena of the inorganic world, there is nothing impossible in this abstraction.

Henceforth, the positive method must adapt itself to the characteristics which belong to biological phenomena. It does not always demand, as it has been wrongly stated, that we should go from the simple to the complex, but only that we should proceed from the known to the unknown. It is true that in the sciences of the inorganic world, we proceed from the least complex to the most complex cases; we begin by the study of phenomena which are as isolated as possible from one another. But, on the contrary, living beings are all the better known to us in proportion as they are more complex. The idea of the animal is in some respects clearer to us than the idea of the vegetable. The idea of the superior animals is clearer to us than that of the inferior ones. Finally man for us is the principal biological unity, and it is from this unity that speculation starts in this science.

Thus, in dealing with Biology the positive method undergoes a veritable inversion. In the preceding sciences, the last degree of composition is forbidden us: we never succeed in uniting the whole of the inorganic world into a single synthesis. In biology, on the contrary, sums of phenomena are given; but it is the last degree of simplicity which escapes us. We have to start from those sums of phenomena, and biology must in this way assume a synthetic character. In it the analysis of phenomena will be as minute as possible; but the analytical operations will always be more or less directly subordinated to the leading idea of the vital *consensus*. . . .

Like the other fundamental sciences Biology must be abstract, that is to say it must not bear upon individual beings, but upon phenomena. It is thus distinct from zoology and botany which are concrete sciences. In its widest generality it is defined through the constant correspondence between the anatomical and the physiological point of view. Its object is to constantly unite them to one another. In reality these two points of view are the two aspects of a single problem. It is owing to historical reasons that, during a certain time, these two sciences appeared to develop independently of one another. Physiology remained attached to the metaphysical methods, that is to say, to unverifiable hypotheses and to principles which went beyond experience, while anatomists already made use of the positive method. But to-day, the two sciences being equally positive, "their opposition is reduced to that which subsists between the static and the dynamic points of view."

Another element which should enter into the more general definition of biology, although it has sometimes been neglected, is the consideration of the *milieu*. The relation between the organism and its *milieu* is no less essential to life than the relation of the organ to the function. Life supposes not only that the being should be organised in a certain way, but also that a certain number of external circumstances should sustain this organisation, and should be compatible with its activity. Living beings are thus dependent upon their *milieu*, and this dependence grows as we rise in the organic series. The system of the conditions of existence becomes all the more complex as the functions develop and become more varied. Inferior organisms are subject to less numerous external conditions; but, says Comte, a little variation in one of these conditions suffices to make them perish. The superior organisms stand a variation of this kind better. But, in return, the number of conditions upon which they depend is far greater. The study of *milieux* in their relations to organisms, a study which is hardly outlined, undoubtedly has many discoveries in store for the future. Here is an order of problems of which Lamarck probably suggested the idea to Comte, and upon which Darwin's genius will work. . . .

What will be the most general problem of the science of life? From the anatomical point of view, says Comte, all possible organisms, all parts whatever of each organism, and all the various states of each necessarily present a common basis of structure and of composition, from which the tissues, organs and apparatus have emerged by means of a progressive differentiation. In the same way, from the physiological point of view, all living beings, from the vegetable kingdom up to man, considered in all their actions and all the periods of their existence, necessarily possess a common basis of vital activity, whence the innumerable phenomena of nutrition, secretion, etc., proceed, by means of progressive differentiation. Now, from both these points of view, that which is similar in these cases is more important than that which distinguishes them, since the more general phenomena govern those which are less so. We must therefore disengage the elementary physiological phenomenon and the anatomical structure which corresponds to it, we must determine their relation, and, with the help and confirmation of experience, we must deduce the increasingly more complex, physiological and anatomical, phenomena from it. . . .

In part, or even entirely, biology is deprived of certain methodical processes which are utilised by the sciences which precede it. It cannot avail itself of calculation. Undoubtedly each of the elements which go to make up a physiological phenomenon varies according to a definite law. But the sum of these elements forms such a complex whole, that we shall never be able to express their relations in the terms of an equation. Further, the numbers which are relative to the phenomena of living bodies present continual and irregular variations, which do not allow us to establish the data of a mathematical calculation. Each living being has its individuality, its personal formula, its characteristic reactions, which prevent us from treating it as identical with the other beings of the same species. Each physiological or pathological "case" is distinct from any other case. That is why Comte distrusts statistics. In his judgment they are misleading in physiology, and fatal in medicine. In the same way, Claude Bernard will protest vigorously against averages. . . .

Experimenting is very difficult in biology, for nothing is easier than to disturb, to suspend, or even to bring about the entire cessation of the phenomena of life. . . .

Nevertheless, as we know, it is not man's intervention in phenomena which constitutes experimenting, properly so called. It consists, before all things, in the rational selection of cases (natural or artificial, it matters little), which are most appropriate for bringing out the law of variation of the phenomenon under observation. Nature gives us such, for illnesses resemble experiments which we can follow through their entire course and to their termination. They are often difficult to interpret, on account of their extreme complexity, but less so, however, than the majority of the experiments which we bring about ourselves. For are they not more or less violent diseases, suddenly produced by our intervention, without our being able to foresee all their indirect and future consequences? It is pathological anatomy which led Bichat to his fine discoveries in histology and in physiology. And to pathology we must join teratology which is, as it were, its prolongation. Here again, nature supplies experiments which we should not know how to institute.

Whatever may be the help which biology derives from these natural ways of experimenting, its progress could only be a very slow one if it did not possess besides a powerful method for proceeding which is peculiar to it: comparison. It is true that every inductive operation implies comparison. We compare what we observe with other real and possible cases. Again we compare when we are experimenting. But, in the comparative method, properly so called, we do not limit ourselves to bringing two cases together. Comparison bears upon a long sequence of analogous cases, in which the subject is modified by a continual succession of almost insensible gradations.

How would the general problems of biology receive a solution without this method? If we consider an organism by itself, the complication of functions and organs is inextricable in it. But, if we compare this organism with those which come nearest to it, and then with others which are near to them and so on, disengaging what they have in common, a simplification is produced. The accessory characteristics disappear by degrees, as we descend in the biological series, and, if we have set ourselves to study a certain function, we can finally determine its relation to its organ. . . .

The comparative method will then apply successively to the different parts of an organism, to the different ages of the same organism, and to the different organisms in the animal and vegetable series. . . . The primitive state of the highest organism, he says, must represent, from the anatomical and physiological point of view, the essential characteristics of the complete state which belongs to the more inferior organism, and so on successively "without our being able to find again the exact analogy of each of the principal terms of the inferior organic series in the sole analysis of the various phases of development of each superior organism." This comparison, so to speak, allows us to realise in the same individual the growing complication of organs and of functions which characterises the whole biological hierarchy. . . .

The problem of classification is . . . an essential part of general biology. In the natural classification sought after by science, the position assigned to each organism would suffice to define at once the whole of its anatomical and physiological nature in relation to the organisms which precede and to those which follow. Any natural classification cannot, however, be anything but imperfect. Accustomed as we are to artificial classifications, which admit of absolute and immediate perfection, we are surprised that the same should not be the case in natural classification. But, if the latter is a real science, we must own that, here as elsewhere, we can only reach more or less distant approximations. The co-ordination of living species is a problem like the static or dynamic analysis of a determined organism. Like this analysis, it only allows of solutions which are approached rather than realised. . . .

It is not surprising that biology, even more than physics and chemistry, preserves the metaphysical spirit. Such, for instance, is the hypothesis of spontaneous generation. Positive philosophy recognizes that each living being always emanates from another similar being. This is not established a priori, but is the result of an "immense induction." Omne vivum ex vivo. Efforts to explain how the generating tissue should itself be formed by kinds of organic monads . . . can only fail. We should never know how to connect the organic with the inorganic world except through the fundamental laws belonging to the general phenomena which are common to them both. Positive speculations in anatomy and in physiology form a limited system, within which we must establish the most perfect unity but which must ever remain separated from the whole of inorganic theories. We see clearly, it is true, that there is no matter which is of itself living. Life is not peculiar to certain substances which are organised in a certain manner. It never belongs to them for more than a time: every organism of which the molecules are not renewed is dissolved. But "we can no more explain this instability than this speciality."

In the same way we see that in living bodies the nutritive functions are the basis of the others; but there is no contradiction in "dreaming" of thought and sociability in beings whose substance would remain unalterable. From this point of view spiritualism is not less admissible than materialism, in so much as death does not seem to be a necessary consequence of life. This again is an idea which is common to Descartes and to Comte. They both conceive an organism in which the play of functions should not cease of itself. The theory of death, says Comte, although it is founded upon that of life, is entirely distinct from it. . . .

By its lower extremity [biology] is contiguous to inorganic science (the physico-chemical phenomena of vegetative life). By its higher extremity (intellectual functions), it reaches to the final science, or sociology. But the adherence is far from being as close in one case as in the other. At the moment when we pass from the inorganic world to the world of living beings, according to positive philosophy, there is a sudden "enrichment of the real." The transition is very marked. The domain of biology is not so sharply separated from that of sociology. For the higher biological functions, the intellectual functions, cannot be analysed from the point of view of the individual, at least in man, but only from the point of view of the species. We must then, while preserving the distinction between the two sciences, admit a kind of inter-relation between them. Undoubtedly sociology could not be founded so long as biology had not made decisive progress. But, conversely, sociology once founded alone completes the positive study of the highest biological functions.

Certainly, biology has not been less transformed than chemistry . . . and the state in which we see it to-day differs singularly from that in which Comte knew it. It has been developed and differentiated far beyond what he could foresee. None the less he conceived some of its principles with remarkable power. He had a precise idea of that which could constitute a general biology, that is, a single physiology and anatomy for the whole of living beings.

8

The Necessity for Sociology

The prestige of science today is so great that we take for granted a universal desire for pursuing it in all spheres. But this desire is not even universal as regards the inorganic and organic sciences in parts of the world where theological or metaphysical ideas hold sway. Through social science and particularly through the impetus of sociology comes a challenge to that power which controls in any part by propagation of myth, by concealment, and by factitious egalitarianism. Comte, for all his optimism, was not unaware of the difficulties in the path of establishing and advancing sociology. The Aristotelian doctrine "All men desire to know" is sociologically incorrect. Men generally desire to know what they have been ordered or compelled or seduced to know. Sociology demands of them that they ask why they are not permitted to know otherwise. In Comte's time, ideological confusion or intellectual chauvinism particularly suited those who lived off the fruits of the labor of others.

By "order," Comte (at least originally) did not mean an authoritarian regime but a code of ethics that men could live by in the new industrial society which had upset the old "order" and left confusion. Order is "the continuous extension of liberty" and "the general expansion of human powers." Paramount here for Comte was the amelioration of the conditions of the lower classes.

Mental reorganization, by habitually interposing a common moral authority between the working classes and the leaders of society, will offer the only regular basis of a pacific and equitable reconciliation of their chief conflicts, nearly abandoned in the present day to the savage discipline of a purely material antagonism.

But this mental reorganization will not come about through the leadership of scientists who deal with inorganic and biological phenomena for they have become too specialized to see the general mo-

68

rality of the philosophical unity which underlies their specialties. Indeed, "the scientific class decrees its own political subordination."

In the Cours, the dogmatism of which John Stuart Mill later accused Comte does not appear, but a remarkably sophisticated attitude towards the wisdom of knowing what we do not know or cannot know does. Men have to resign themselves to those shortcomings which arise from human limitations. We cannot cure all political evils, for power to one degree or another always corrupts. Trained sociologists will inform men of what they do not know but this learned ignorance can only come about by discovering the laws of social phenomena. Progress is not certainty but the lessening of uncertainty. Sociology leads to good will, sacrifice, fellow-feeling, and the triumph of the heart over the shortcomings of the intellect. Catholicism erred finally by distorting the emotions through torturing reason, Protestantism by making material considerations paramount.

The necessity for sociology is coordinate with its becoming an abstract science, that is, a science of phenomena and not merely a science of factual interconnection. Concrete sciences will inform us about the factual world, but abstract science will teach men how to live, since its aim is the transformation of the external world rather than its crude acceptance. Abstract science is the humanization of the concrete sciences which are preludes to it or partial developments of it. And so the philosophical unity upon which humanist regeneration rests is the discovery of the beliefs common to all the concrete sciences—beliefs which teach men how to live in peace.

No greater task has ever been set for sociology than the one set by its founder. For Comte, contemporary empirical sociology would present a sorry sight, for with its concentration on the discovery of concrete laws its practitioners are led into the very political subordination which has plagued inorganic and organic scientists. Abstract science is a morality whereas concrete science is only an explanation of the inadequate world whose control so pitilessly deludes men into inappropriate relationships with each other. It is significant that earlier American sociologists (for example, Ward, Small, and Cooley) were led by somewhat different paths to the same conclusion as Comte whereas later and recent American empiricists (such as George Lundberg) have been led to opposite conclusions, all the while proclaiming themselves to be positivists and even followers and adherents of Auguste Comte. Such is the irony of sociology, that these latter claim to be followers of the man who would be the first to disown them as distorters of his doctrine.

Comte discusses the indispensability of sociology in Positive Philosophy, pp. 399–400, and order and progress on pp. 432–38. He discusses the union of feeling and reason on pp. 11–13, and the relation of abstract to concrete laws on pp. 30–32 of Vol. I of Positive Polity.

9

Psychology and Sociology

Comte's early opposition (amounting almost to contempt) for what was called "psychology" in his day caused him to refuse to admit such a subject into his classification of the basic sciences. Among other things, he found it too rationalistic in considering man as essentially a reasoning animal, too introspective in depending upon non-clinical self-observation, and too metaphysical in being tied to certain speculative theories of knowledge. The problems, however, that the psychologists dealt with were real problems, and in the Cours, Comte tries to deal with them as part of what he calls cerebral biology or cerebral physiology.

By the time he turned to the writing of Positive Polity, a new perspective set in—a highly humanistic perspective. He was then faced with the principle that the emotions which make up "human nature" are everywhere the same but are expressed differently through the varying milieux. The study of these variations became the center of his sociology. Sociological inspiration, he wrote, must be controlled by zoological [psychological] appreciation. The subjective method in sociology must be a positivist subjective method which could show how man's emotions become socialized.

Though based on the instincts, Comte's psychology is historical in that it takes as its problem the demonstration of why the instincts in a given milieu express themselves the way they do. Comte put it plainly, "The nature of man evolves without being transformed." Psychology becomes for the later Comte not merely a department of sociology but the largest part of it. He himself tells us so in volume three of Positive Polity. Following up Comte's thought, Lévy-Bruhl forthrightly announces:

In a word, the chief regulator of sociology is the science of human nature. It can even be said, without forcing the meaning of Comte's

71

thought, that sociology is really a psychology, not indeed, it is true, a
psychology founded upon the introspective analysis of the individual
subject, but a psychology whose object is the analysis of history, of the
universal subject, that is to say, of Humanity.

*Though Comte could not understand the instincts as psychoanaly-
sis did later, his perceptions are classical forerunners. He understands
that there is an ongoing battle between the primitive instincts and
socialization, that the instincts (which he subsumes under the
general terms "will" or "desire") remain preponderant and are
the founts of action, that thought is filled with what today we would
call rationalization, and that sublimation of frustrated instincts and
of repressed aggression is indispensable to human development. His
analyses here are not simply guesswork but the result of deep emotional experiences in his own life. But where Freud saw the discon-
tents of civilization, Comte saw the triumph of the Religion of
Humanity; where Freud was agnostic, Comte was religious though
not theological. There is undoubtedly a trend of thought which runs
from Comte to Freud but it has not yet been explored. Comte knew
of the work of the neuro-pathologists of his time and appreciated it.
One common fact with regard to general public and even professional sociological opinion concerning both Comte and Freud does
stand out rather boldly—neither one is known in his own words as
widely as their names are bruited about and both of them have suffered heinous misunderstanding from the overwhelming majority of
sociologists.*

1. The Instincts

Self-interest of the direct kind, the primary and fundamental form
of Egoism, may be divided into the instincts of Preservation and of
Improvement. The first of these is obviously the most energetic and
the most universal. It is at once less noble and more indispensable
than any other. We find it under one form or other in the lowest of
the animals, which but for it would very soon perish. But it is
rarely that this predominant instinct is found unmixed, and the
ordinary conception of it as such is vague and confused. The positive
conception distinguishes the tendency to preserve the Individual

SOURCE: *Positive Polity*, Vol. I, pp. 560–69.

from the tendency to preserve the Race. To the biologist the separation of the two instincts will be evident enough, since in the lowest part of the animal scale, where the sexes are not entirely separate, the second instinct is not perceptible. . . . The first is called the *Nutritive* instinct, Nutrition being its principal attribute. But it should always be borne in mind that besides nutrition it includes all that relates directly to the material preservation of the individual. It is the only instinct which is strictly universal, no animal supporting life without it. Even in the human race it is the foundation on which all the others are raised. . . .

And yet Gall omitted this instinct altogether. Perhaps indeed the very fact of its predominance induced him to give way to the old physiological prejudice that it could not be fixed in any special site. But it is only in the lowest grade of the animal scale, where all anatomical distinction is lost in perfect homogeneity, that such an organ is likely to be wanting. Everywhere else we should expect to find it; and its importance will increase as the animal is higher in the scale, because the propensities become more various, and their divergent forces would distract attention from self-preservation were there not a special organ appropriated to it. Gall's successors have indeed looked for it, but in a confused and empirical way. . . .

We come now to the preservation of the Race. Here we have obviously two separate instincts, the sexual and the maternal; the former being superior in energy, inferior in dignity. Throughout the animal scale we find the distinction between them clearly marked. We have cases where there is perfect separation of the sexes, and yet but little care for the offspring. Gall appears to me to have been right in his opinion of their situation, with the exception of the alteration which I have just introduced. His localisation conforms here to the subjective Method, which obviously would have pointed, even without his aid, to the same result.

Here then we have in detail the three first terms of the affective series; that is to say, the three instincts of preservation, nutritive, sexual, and maternal. The increasing rank and decreasing energy on which the classification depends are here very clearly marked. . . . The continuity of action, which I have already spoken of as common to the whole affective region, obtains unquestionably in the first of these three instincts. The solicitude for self-preservation is unremitting. The other two, though at first sight seeming intermittent, will not be so regarded when we look at the cases where their action is not thwarted by external restraint. When the natural satisfaction of the instinct is impeded, as is often the case, it does not, in the higher races at least, cease to act, but simply seeks another issue.

Succeeding to the series of preservative instincts, we have two of a more elevated and less universal kind; the instincts of Improvement. I have named them . . . the *Military* and the *Industrial* instincts, giving a more systematic and extended meaning to terms hitherto limited to human affairs. Higher and less energetic than the preceding, they are more directly concerned with the animal functions, whereas the former were principally concerned with vegetal life. They belong, nevertheless, like those, to the egoistic division; since in stimulating the animal to ameliorate his condition they appeal only to self-gratification. Such amelioration may be attained by either of two ways, which often co-exist: by the destruction of obstacles, or by the construction of instruments. The first mode is by no means confined, as might be supposed, to the carnivorous races. On the contrary, it is more universal than the second, being at once more indispensable and more easy. No animal, whether herbivorous or carnivorous, can exist without destroying many of the objects round it; and not merely inanimate but animate objects, sometimes indeed, as in the case of sexual combats, beings of its own species. Spurzheim showed sound judgment in generalising the conception of this instinct, which by Gall had been restricted to its more salient manifestations. The Industrial instinct is more rare, and is less obvious. Yet it is sufficiently prevalent throughout the animal kingdom to be incorporated into the biological treatment of the subject. True, it is only in the human race that it is fully developed. But the same thing really may be said of the Military instinct. In no other race does War result in permanent conquest, even of an individual kind. The constructive instinct, like the Social, has been too much limited to a few exceptional species, which would seem to be dispersed arbitrarily through the animal kingdom. But in one form or other it should exist in every case where the instincts of preservation, especially the maternal instinct, render special operations necessary. The meaning hitherto attached to it has been too restricted. It should include every sort of tendency leading in the direction of amelioration of condition; and such tendencies must very often be estimated quite apart from actual results, most of the constructive animals being much hampered in their efforts, principally by man's interference. . . .

Having fixed the arrangement and position of the five egoistic instincts, it becomes easy to extend the series to those intermediate propensities which lead us ultimately by a gradual transition to the social instincts. The transition consists of two affections which, though often confounded, are yet very distinct: Pride, or the love of Power; and Vanity, or the love of Approbation. Both are essentially personal, whether in their origin or in their object. But the means through which these instincts are to be gratified give them a social character, and render their tendencies far more modifiable than those which we have been just considering, not merely in the case of Man, but in that of other races. There is, however, a considerable difference between them in this respect. Vanity, as Gall very clearly perceived, is to be ranked above Pride. The facility with which it is modified by external influences is indeed so marked as to lead some thinkers very erroneously to credit it with originating the social instinct, which on the contrary it presupposes. A comprehensive glance at the animal kingdom is all that is needed to correct this elementary mistake, so mischievous in its moral consequences. In the case of Man, the distinction between these two intermediate propensities may be looked upon as the first natural origin of the division between the two social powers. . . . Each of these instincts aims alike at personal ascendancy; but the one aims at it by force, the other by opinion. Pride therefore seeks positions of command; Vanity seeks the consultative influence of conviction or persuasion. Now, as I have already explained in the General View, this essentially corresponds with the permanent distinction between the temporal and spiritual powers. . . .

We have now to consider the culminating point of the affective series; the social or altruistic propensities, towards which the preceding terms of the series have been gradually leading us. The increase in dignity and decrease in energy, which have formed throughout our principle of classification, are here in full prominence. But there is a certain compensation for their inferiority of force in their natural capability for more complete development, since they can be shared by all simultaneously, not merely without antagonism, but with an increase of pleasure resulting from such community of feeling. Although, as I have already explained, it is only in our own race that this characteristic property can be fully manifested, its first appearance should be noted in Biology, as the best preparation for examining it afterwards more thoroughly in Sociology. That these

higher instincts are shared by many animal species is beyond question. They exist sometimes in a higher degree of intensity than in
Man; and independently of this they are not complicated with social
institutions and intellectual influences. Here consequently it is that
their true character can be rigorously defined, so as to leave no room
for uncertainty. Without the aid afforded by the observation of
animals, our feeble reasoning powers would never have been able to
withstand the sophistical attempts of theology and ontology to dis-
prove the existence of innate sympathetic instincts; and indeed they
still remain unacknowledged by minds who reject the validity of this
appeal.

The principal tendency of these higher propensities is in the direction of a complete revolution in the mode of attaining Vital Unity.
In a complicated organism the harmony of the whole must always
depend upon adequate subordination of all spontaneous impulses to
one preponderating principle. Now such a principle may either be
egoist or altruist. Hence the distinction already mentioned between
the two modes of establishing the vital consensus. The second of
these modes surpasses the first, as being the only one compatible with
the social state. But more than this, the unity attained by it is, even
from the individual aspect, more complete, more easy, and more
permanent. The lower instincts derive their incentives to conduct
from purely individual sources; and as these are both numerous and
varied in character they are incompatible with any fixity of action, or
even with any permanence of character, except during the periodic
activity to which each of the stronger appetites is in turn excited.
The individual must subordinate himself to an Existence outside itself in order to find in it the source of his own stability. And this
condition cannot be effectually realised except under the impulse of
propensities prompting him to live for others. The being, whether
man or animal, who loves nothing outside himself, and really lives
for himself alone, is by that very fact condemned to pass his life in
a miserable alternation of ignoble torpor and uncontrolled excitement. Evidently the principal feature of Progress in all living things
is that the general consensus which we have seen to be the essential
attribute of vitality should become more perfect. It follows that
happiness and worth, as well in individuals as in societies, depend on
adequate ascendancy of the sympathetic instincts. Thus the expression, *Live for Others*, is the simplest summary of the whole moral
code of Positivism. . . .

None but our own race, as I have already explained, can bring this constitution of things to full maturity, by the establishment of Sociocracy as the result of a long course of probation, which for the advanced part of humanity is now complete. Still, many other races might reach a similar result by exchanging savage independence for voluntary subjection, as is the case already with those whose organisation is specially favourable to it. Thus a vast Biocracy will gradually arise; and its extension to all species susceptible of discipline will be one of the principal results of the moral and social regeneration of mankind. The affiliation of these lower races implies their possession of affections identical with those which, more highly developed, or working under more favourable conditions, lie at the root of human sociability. These nobler instincts tend therefore to become preponderant in all animals capable of subjecting themselves to Man, though such subjection has often been absurdly attributed to slavish fear.

These higher propensities are few in number: to attempt however to reduce them to one would be to fall back into the metaphysical confusion from which Gall has delivered us. He distinguished with great clearness three instincts, requiring merely a more systematic conception of their functions: Attachment, Veneration, and lastly, Goodness or universal Love, the feeling imperfectly represented by theologians under the name of Christian Charity. The natural arrangement of this group, agreeing obviously with our general principle of Classification, terminates the affective series. Like all the preceding groups, we reach it through a process of binary decomposition. The primary division of the sympathetic instincts evidently turns on the special or general character of their aim. In the first case they will be more intense but less noble. This is why they have been spoken of slightingly under the title of collective egoism, an irrational and exaggerated expression, showing a thorough misunderstanding of their essential and permanent feature, the tendency to live for others. But in this first division are comprised two propensities which, as they differ in their degree of speciality, it is important clearly to distinguish. The word Attachment, given by common consent to the first of these, is admirably chosen, indicating as it does the greater energy of the more limited affection. Its full force is only felt when it binds two individuals together. The life of the family is a sufficient and indeed is the most suitable sphere for its action. Consequently we find it highly developed among animals, and often to an even higher degree than in Man. It leads them in many cases to monogamy, reaching sometimes to the ultimate point

of widowhood. The second of the two special sympathies is Veneration, properly so called. The object of this instinct is always definite,
but admits of far wider scope than that of which we have been speaking. Its essential characteristic is voluntary submission. It is therefore
principally manifested towards superiors, whereas the previous instinct operates between equals. We find this noble feeling in many
of the animals, although less frequently than simple attachment.
Some even carry it to the point of worship of the dead, as in many
recorded instances of dogs and their masters. Gall, whose combative
life was not favourable to the exercise of this instinct, had but a
very imperfect understanding of its nature. It was more successfully
handled by Spurzheim, and especially by Broussais, who crowned
his noble career so honourably by the conscientious energy with which
he studied and disseminated a doctrine which he had previously misunderstood. This important instinct forms a natural transition between individual Attachment and universal Love. This last is the
supreme term of the affective series. It admits of many degrees, but
is not divisible into any other, being characterised by the collective nature of its aim, whatever the extent of the collection. From
the love of the tribe or community to the widest patriotism, or to
sympathy with all beings who can be brought to share a common
life, the feeling never alters in character. Only it becomes at once
weaker and more elevated as it extends more widely, following the
law common to the whole affective series. Animals have it in a less
degree than the other two sympathetic propensities. It should not
however be looked upon as an exclusive attribute of our race, though
it forms its most distinguishing characteristic. By a happy ambiguity
of language the same expression is used to designate the widest
exercise of this highest affection, and also the race in whom it exists
to the highest degree. And as in this fullest sense it is incompatible
with any feeling of hatred to other races, there is little inconvenience
in using the term as the expression of the largest and most universal
form of sympathy. The reader will therefore understand my motive
in applying the name of Humanity . . . to the best type of vital
unity, which, as the foregoing remarks will have shown, tends more
and more towards dependence upon this instinct.

Before leaving the analysis of this group, which brings the Affective series to a close, I must not omit to notice its profound ethical
importance. It is of course a less dangerous mistake to confound all
the social sympathies in one than to ignore their existence altogether.
But this vague mode of regarding them is inadequate in theory and

is still more mischievous in practice. It leads indeed sometimes to most subversive consequences, as may be seen but too clearly in the present state of the human race; the advanced portion of it being led by this error into the most dangerous aberrations, both private and public. It would be out of place to develop this thought at present; I only mention it to show the great service rendered by systematic biology in demonstrating the natural source of that education of the feelings on which the whole discipline of our race depends. When studied in the animal kingdom, the separation and progression of these sympathies become evident to the most obstinate of metaphysicians. Not merely must he acknowledge the distinction in name, but also the gradation in dignity and in energy, and farther, what is extremely important, their succession in time. Building on this foundation, Sociology is the better able afterwards to show the folly and danger of tendencies which ruin the whole training of the affections, by aiming at once and without preparation at the highest of the sympathies, instead of regarding it merely as the final term.

10

Social Statics

The two main divisions of sociology for Comte are "social statics" and "social dynamics." Statics is the part which deals with the laws of human social existence embedded in the conditions of a society, and it betokens the realm of order. On the other hand, dynamics deals with the laws of social movement or social change. They clearly intertwine, but for purposes of exposition Comte treats the laws of human order in the abstract, disavowing all questions of movement.

Though the individual is basic to all social life, social statics deals with him as an abstraction and stresses the cooperation of individuals that creates consensus. Thus, the individual—a bundle of instincts of which the personal (the egoistic) are unsocial, or asocial, or even antisocial—is treated as a social being, a group representative, but one who can challenge and change the collectivity. This treatment is, moreover, justified by the empirical situation, that is, that there is no state of nature but only a state of human nature which is social. For Comte, Rousseau was a dreary romantic. Men do not contract into society, they are born in and of it. Or as Lévy-Bruhl writes:

The idea of the social *consensus*, more restricted than that of the vital consensus, dominates the whole of social statics. The science sets itself to study the continual actions and reactions which the various parts of the social system exercise upon one another. Each of the numerous elements of this system, instead of being observed by itself, must be conceived as in relation with all the others, with which it has constant solidarity. From whatever social element we start, it is always connected, in a more or less direct way, with the whole of the others, even with those which at first sight appear independent.

The family is the basic social unit and marriage is the fundamental institution. But the family is not society. Society demands the co-operation of families. Man is not naturally cooperative; cooperation is a derivative of interfamilial coordination. In modern society, cooperation is based on the division of labor and this division of labor is the foundation of the modern form taken by society. From it comes solidarity through mutual need and from the advanced forms of the division of labor comes the complexity of the contemporary social organism. But responsible government is indispensable to the felicitous operation of the division of labor. Moreover, division of labor differentiates individuals and leads to moral and intellectual change as men come to have more and more need of each other. Differentiation has its negative aspect by widening the separation of interests and leading to dissensus or organizational anomy. This anomy requires the intervention of government to reestablish the consensus that has broken down.

Thus, government is not a necessary evil but a positive force for achieving a continually shifting consensus. For its bureaucratic forms Comte had nothing but scorn; but these forms arise from the complexity of modern political organization. Government does basically work for social cohesion. Comte describes the collective representations which make such cohesion possible—internalized beliefs which become components of a generalized ideology. Human society owes its continuance, therefore, to the internalization of a community of beliefs and sentiments; though society seems beyond the individual, it can persist only through the general internal acceptance by individuals of its codes and regulations. This harmony of interests rests on what Comte considers to be religious feelings. In the Polity, Comte goes further. He discusses the necessity for a community of beliefs (humanitarian, not theological). These beliefs are fundamental to economic life, the family, language, government, voluntary associations—in short, to general social solidarity which persists even amidst changes occurring in a given society.

Comte came to see that a science of human society could not only answer the question "What is man?" but also the question "How should he lead his life?" In Positive Polity, the second question—"How should man lead his life?"—becomes primary and Comte reaches the conclusion that man can be what he ought to be only by following an ideal of humanity adapted to the emergent conditions and determinants of modern industrial society. So, religion which seems at first to be involved basically in social statics becomes dynamic —a Religion of Humanity that can consolidate a new consensus by applying a humanist ethic appropriate to industrial life.

1. Social Statics as the Abstract Theory of Social Laws

It is necessary to resolve the positive study of Humanity into two essential parts. The one, the statical, will treat of the structural nature of this, the chief of organisms; the other, the dynamical, will treat the laws of its actual development. . . . The study of social Statics is at once more simple, more general, and more abstract, than that of social Dynamics. Moreover social Statics form the direct link between the final science of Society and the whole of the preceding sciences, and in a special manner between the final science and Biology, of which Sociology now bcomes the natural complement. Unless based upon a sound theory of the laws of its *existence*, or fixed organic conditions, the study of the *movement*, or organic evolution, of human society would fall short of that scientific coherence, needed for this study to attain to its full usefulness. Nor is this distinction of less importance in practice than it is in theory; for the dynamical laws find their chief application in politics, the statical, in morals.

Between these two classes of social laws there reigns a sovereign spirit of harmony, by virtue of the general principle, which here, as elsewhere, combines the study of Movement, with that of the Existence. The value of this principle was first seen in the field of mere mathematics; but it is in Sociology where its full importance and character will be finally displayed. Here its proper part is to picture Progress as nothing but the gradual development of Order. Conversely it represents to us Order as manifested forth by Progress. . . . In Biology we now regard all forms of life simply as an evolution, and we discard any notion of creation in the proper sense of that word. But this great axiom of science has especially its place in Sociology; where studying a course of development yet more complex, more extensive, and more gradual, we are forced to recognise the fundamental unity which runs through all the successive phases. In this science the statical study, and the dynamical study tend gradually to unite in one, as the essential spirit of each more and more distinctly comes out, to illustrate the intimate connection between

SOURCE: *Positive Polity*, Vol. II, pp. 1-3, 384-87.

hem; and we explain alternately the laws of Order by those of
Progress, and the laws of Progress by those of Order. . . .

The statical method alone can give a really solid basis to a sound
Social Philosophy, first because it connects it more closely with the
entire range of Natural Philosophy, secondly because it reduces the
constituent elements of Social Philosophy to a more truly systematic
form. For this special object then I shall consider the laws of human
Order in the abstract, discarding all question of movement as if that
Order was fixed. We shall thus ascertain the primary laws of Society
which are necessarily common to all times, and to all places. This
will afford a scientific foundation for the treatment of the gradual
course of human development, which has been nothing but the
growing fulfilment of that System of Life, best adapted to man,
whereof the essential form from the first has existed in germ. . . .

The scheme . . . may be summed up and illustrated by simply
tracing the history of the elementary term of Statics; inasmuch as
Language has an inherent tendency to reflect man's entire nature.
If we compare the two general senses of the word, Order, we find
that it always connotes at the same time commandment and arrangement. During the whole course of previous civilisation, the purpose
of which was rather to develop man's various forces than to regulate
them, Command was thought more important than Arrangement;
and indeed Arrangement could not even begin in any other way, for
want of an external base. The adult state of Man, on the other hand,
is distinguished by the higher importance of Arrangement; when,
Order being directly founded upon its objective type in External
Nature, it merely requires Command as a subsidiary instrument,
wherewith to turn our decisions into practical action. Thus the contrast between the Absolute synthesis and the Relative synthesis may
be represented as the mere reversing of the places held, now by one,
and now by the other sense of the word, Order. In fact the inversion
which is thus naturally brought about between Command and Arrangement is at once a formula to express the fact: that Laws have
taken the place of Causes; and an indication of the growing tendency
to make Spiritual Discipline of higher import than Temporal Government.

It might be thought that the fundamental laws of Human
Order would be sufficient to give a systematic form to the destiny
of man: which must ever consist in a closer approach to the primary type. But we may gather from all that has been said . . .

that, however necessary is this body of theory, it is in no way all
that we require; for it has left undetermined the manner, and the
time, in which the typical Order may ultimately come about, simply
explaining the conditions which inevitably prepare the way. The
most complete Statical theory therefore is never adequate as a guide
to social action; although it is always an element necessary for
action. To rely upon the Statical type alone, or even too largely
would usually involve us in serious mischief; for it would give to our
political designs too absolute a character, and too vague a direction. . . .

Amongst numberless examples which history can supply of dangerous illusions due to the use of Statical views without their
dynamic corrective, it is enough to mention how all the great men
of antiquity utterly misconceived the gain to civilisation, which
the Middle Age had in store. . . . The best spirits of the ancient
world long committed the blunder of rejecting Catholicism in its
birth, as it seemed to them to be directly diverting Humanity
from the noble social end which towards the close of antiquity
seemed to be opening to mankind. Now we can easily perceive how
this mistake, inevitable as it was, was produced; it was owing to
their complete ignorance of any historical movement, which could
enable them to see the necessary stages through which they must
pass in order to reach this Statical Type. From the time of Scipio
and Cæsar down to Trajan and Constantine, philosophers and
statesmen were both coming more and more to perceive, how the
entire advance of the whole Roman world was implanting Positive knowledge in place of Theological or Metaphysical creeds,
and Industrial activity in place of a life of War. But, as they had
no clear Knowledge of human Progress, they utterly failed to see
how necessary to civilisation was the stage of Monotheism and of
Feudalism. The best amongst them were thus too often led to
sully their names by savage persecution of the Christians, who
unconsciously were working out the lofty Organisation of Life,
towards which also the greater Romans were struggling after an
abstract, and therefore impossible, type.

Such a catastrophe may warn us how urgent is the need for
the true Philosophy of History, for want of which the Intelligence
of modern times may again think it necessary to break with the
Past, and for fifteen centuries to seek a new course for human
progress. It is true that in the act of conceiving aright the normal
order in social Statics, we make a necessary approach to the period

of its actual advent; for the imagination never can be very far in advance of reality, especially in such a case as the ultimate state of Humanity.

2. *Human Nature and Social Statics*

Passing over some elementary considerations which belong rather to a special treatise on . . . physiological conditions—such as the natural nakedness of the human being, and his helpless and protracted infancy—which have been much exaggerated as social influences, since they exist in some animal races without producing the same social consequences—I proceed to estimate the influence of the most important attributes of our nature in giving to society the fundamental character which belongs to it, and which remains permanent through all degrees of its development. In this view, the first consideration is of the preponderance of the affective over the intellectual faculties, which, though less remarkable in Man than in other animals, yet fixes the first essential idea of our true nature.—Though continuous action is, in all cases, an indispensable condition of success, Man, like every other animal, has a natural dislike to such perseverance, and at first finds pleasure only in a varied exercise of his activity—the variety being of more importance to him than moderation in degree—especially in the commonest cases, in which no strongly-marked instinct is concerned. The intellectual faculties being naturally the least energetic, their activity, if ever so little protracted beyond a certain degree, occasions in most men a fatigue which soon becomes utterly insupportable; and it is in regard to them chiefly that men of all ages of civilization relish that state of which the *dolce far niente* is the most perfect expression. Nevertheless, it is on the persevering use of these high faculties that the modifications of human life, general and individual, depend, during the course of our social development, so that we are met at once by the melancholy coincidence that Man is most in need of precisely the kind of activity for which he is the least fit. . . .

The second consideration is that, besides the preponderance of the affective over the intellectual life, the lowest and most personal propensities have, in regard to social relations, an unquestionable

SOURCE: *Positive Philosophy*, pp. 499–502.

preponderance over the nobler. According to the sound biological theory of man, our social affections are inferior in strength and steadiness to the personal, though the common welfare must depend especially on the regular satisfaction of the former, which first originate the social state for us, and then maintain it against the divergences of individual instincts. To understand the sociological value of this biological datum, we must observe, as in the former case, that the condition is necessary, and that it is only its degree that we have to deplore. . . . The reciprocal connection of those two chief moderators of human life, intellectual activity and the social instinct, seems thus to be unquestionable: and the first function of universal morals, in regard to the individual, consists in increasing this double influence, the gradual extension of which constitutes the first spontaneous result of the general development of humanity. And the double opposition between Man's moral and material need of intellectual toil and his dislike of it, and again, between Man's need, for his own happiness, of the social affections, and the necessary subjection of these to his personal instincts, discloses the scientific germ of the struggle . . . between the conservative and the reforming spirit; the first of which is animated by purely personal instincts, and the other by the spontaneous combination of intellectual activity with the various social instincts.

11

Social Dynamics

As distinct from social statics, Comte's social dynamics study the laws of progress. These laws have as indispensable limiting conditions the action of man upon his environment, and the power of the instincts and their socialization to the point where man can plan his own social life. Progress is by fits and starts but inevitable. It is spurred on by ennui and the desire for novelty, somewhat impeded by the limited duration of individual human lives, and accelerated by increase of population.

Progress arises from continuous cooperation ending in benevolence. This benevolence is tied in with the development of the sciences and is ultimately attained through the most complex of them— sociology. Of all phenomena, the social are most modifiable as man learns more and more about himself. But long eras of military conquest and theocratic rule and several series of compromises with metaphysics pass before humanity can realize pacific existence in an industrial milieu.

The dynamics of progress finally achieve a new statical state which in turn will generate its own dynamism. Man looks for stability through change. This change is limited in intensity and speed by attempts to keep order while pursuing progress. When the drive for progress outruns the ability to modify the formerly statical conditions of existence, revolutions will ensue but they will be abortive. But when the possibility for modification of conditions is ignored, revolutions will ensue which will ultimately be successful and a new compromise between order and progress is then inevitable. The vanguard of these revolutions must be positivists who understand the laws of social life and set humanitarian goals for all men. Progress is the story of assimilation of dynamic elements into a new statical order—assimilation spurred on by advances in the use

of reason (philosophy) and marked by the ongoing struggle for
the supremacy of positivism.

1. Aspects of the Theory of the Natural Progress
of Human Society

Civilization develops, to an enormous degree, the action of Man
upon his environment: and thus, it may seem, at first, to concentrate
our attention upon the cares of material existence, the support and
improvement of which appear to be the chief object of most social
occupations. A closer examination will show, however, that this
development gives the advantage to the highest human faculties,
both by the security which sets free our attention from physical
wants, and by the direct and steady excitement which it administers
to the intellectual functions, and even the social feelings. In Man's
social infancy, the instincts of subsistence are so preponderant, that
the sexual instinct itself, notwithstanding its primitive strength, is
at first controlled by them: the domestic affections are then much
less pronounced; and the social affections are restricted to an almost
imperceptible fraction of humanity, beyond which everything is
foreign, and even hostile; and the malignant passions are certainly,
next to the animal appetites, the mainspring of human existence. It
is unquestionable that civilization leads us on to a further and further
development of our noblest dispositions and our most generous
feelings, which are the only possible basis of human association,
and which receive, by means of that association, a more and more
special culture. As for the intellectual faculties—we see, by the
habitual improvidence which characterizes savage life, how little
influence reason has over men in that stage of existence. Those
faculties are then undeveloped, or show some activity only in the
lowest order, which relate to the exercise of the senses: the faculties of abstraction and combination are almost wholly inert, except
under some transient stimulus: the rude curiosity which the spectacle of nature involuntarily inspires is quite satisfied with the
weakest attempts at theological explanation; and amusements,
chiefly distinguished by violent muscular activity, rising at best to
a manifestation of merely physical address, are as little favorable

SOURCE: *Positive Philosophy*, pp. 516–22, 537–40.

to the development of intelligence as of social qualities. The influence of civilization in perpetually improving the intellectual faculties is even more unquestionable than its effect on moral relations. The development of the individual exhibits to us in little, both as to time and degree, the chief phases of social development. In both cases, the end is to subordinate the satisfaction of the personal instincts to the habitual exercise of the social faculties, subjecting, at the same time, all our passions to rules imposed by an ever-strengthening intelligence, with the view of identifying the individual more and more with the species. In the anatomical view, we should say that the process is to give an influence by exercise to the organs of the cerebral systems, increasing in proportion to their distance from the vertebral column, and their nearness to the frontal region. Such is the ideal type which exhibits the course of human development, in the individual, and, in a higher degree, in the species. This view enables us to discriminate the natural from the artificial part of the process of development; that part being natural which raises the human to a superiority over the animal attributes; and that part being artificial by which any faculty is made to preponderate in proportion to its original weakness: and here we find the scientific explanation of that eternal struggle between our humanity and our animality which has been recognised by all who have made Man their study, from the earliest days of civilization till now, and embodied in many forms before its true character was fixed by the positive philosophy.

This, then, is the direction of the human evolution. The next consideration is the rate at which it proceeds, apart from any differences which may result from climate, race, or other modifying causes. Taking into the account only universal causes, it is clear that the speed must be in proportion to the combined influence of the chief natural conditions relating to the human organism first, and next to its medium. The invariableness—the evident impossibility of suspending these fundamental conditions must ever prevent our estimating their respective importance, though we may have a general conviction that our spontaneous development must be hastened or retarded by any change in these elementary influences, organic or inorganic; supposing, for instance, our cerebral system to be slightly inferior, in the frontal region; or our planet to become larger or more habitable. Sociological analysis can, by its nature, reach only to accessory conditions, which are rendered susceptible of estimate by their variations.

Among these secondary but permanent influences, which affect the rate of human development, ennui is the first which presents itself. Man, like other animals, can not be happy without a sufficient exercise of all his faculties, intense and persistent in proportion to the intrinsic activity of each faculty. The greater difficulty experienced by man in obtaining a development compatible with the special superiority of his nature renders him more subject than the other animals to that remarkable state of irksome languor which indicates at once the existence of the faculties and their insufficient activity, and which would become equally irreconcilable with a radical debility incapable of any urgent tendency, and with an ideal vigor, spontaneously susceptible of indefatigable exercise. A disposition at once intellectual and moral, which we daily see at work in nature endowed with any energy, must have powerfully accelerated the human expansion, in the infancy of humanity, by the uneasy excitement it occasioned either in the eager search for new sources of emotion, or in the more intense development of direct human activity. This secondary influence is not very marked till the social state is sufficiently advanced to make men feel a growing need to exercise the highest faculties, which are, as we have seen, the least energetic. The strongest faculties, which are the lowest, are so easily exercised that in ordinary circumstances they can hardly generate the ennui which would produce a favorable cerebral reaction. Savages, like children, are not subject to much ennui while their physical activity, which alone is of any importance to them, is not interfered with. An easy and protracted sleep prevents them, as if they were animals, from feeling their intellectual torpor in any irksome way. This brief notice of the influence of ennui was necessary, to show what its operation really amounts to in accelerating the speed of our social evolution. But perhaps the most important of all accelerating influences is the ordinary duration of human life, which I mention in the second place. There is no denying that our social progression rests upon death. I mean, the successive steps suppose the steady renewal of the agents of the general movement, which is almost imperceptible in the course of any single life, and becomes marked only on the succession of a new generation. Here again the social resembles the individual organism— being under the same necessity to throw off its constituent parts as they become, by the vital action itself, unfit for further use, and must be replaced by new elements. To illustrate this, we need not go so far as to suppose an indefinite duration of human life, which would presently put a stop to all progression whatever. It is enough to imagine it lengthened tenfold only, its respective periods preserving their present proportions. If the general constitution of the brain remained the same as now, there must be a retardation; though we know not how great, in our social development: for the perpetual conflict which goes on between the conservative instinct that belongs to age and the innovating instinct which distinguishes youth would be much more favorable than now to the former. From the extreme imperfection of the higher parts of our nature, even those who, in their prime, have contributed most to human progress can not preserve their due social eminence very long without becoming more or less hostile to the further progress which they can not assist. But an ephemeral life would be quite as mischievous as a too protracted one, by giving too much power to the instinct of innovation. The resistance which this instinct now meets with from the conservatism of age compels it to accommodate its efforts to the whole of what has been already done. Without this check, our feeble nature, which has a strong repugnance to irksome and continuous labor, would be for ever proposing incomplete views and crude attempts, that could never ripen into mature projects and feasible acts: and this would be the inevitable state of things, if human life were reduced to a quarter, or even to half its present length. Such would be the consequences, in either case, if we suppose the constitution of the human brain to be much what it is now: and to suppose it essentially changed would be to carry us over into the region of hypothesis.

No justification is however afforded by these considerations to the optimism of the advocates of final causes: for if, in this as in every other case, the actual order is necessarily more or less accordant with the course of the phenomena, it is very far from being true that the arrangement of the natural economy is as good for its purposes as we can easily conceive. The slowness of our social development is no doubt partly owing to the extreme imperfection of our organism; but it is owing nearly as much to the brevity of human life: and there would be no risk to any other great arrangement if the duration of our life, while still limited by the conditions just specified, were doubled or trebled. We have hardly thirty years (and those beset with impediments) to devote to other purposes than preparation for life or for death; and this is a very insufficient balance between what Man can devise and what he can execute. Probably no one has ever nobly devoted himself to the direct advancement of the human mind without bitterly feeling how time, employed to the utmost, failed him for the working out of more than an insignificant part of his conceptions. It will not do to say that the rapid succession of coadjutors compensates for this restriction of individual activity. Important as this compensation is, it is very imperfect, both on account of the loss of time in preparing each successor, and because the precise continuance of the work by different persons, occupying different points of view, is impossible, and the more out of the question exactly in proportion to the value of the new coadjutors. In the simplest material operations, no man's work has ever been carried on by others precisely as he would have done it himself; and the more difficult and lofty labors, which require intellectual and moral forces to complete them, are much more in need of a persistent unity in their management. These intellectual and moral forces no more admit of partition and addition by successors than by contemporaries; and, whatever the advocates of the indefinite distribution of individual efforts may say, a certain degree of concentration is necessary to the accomplishment of human progress.

Another cause which affects the rate of progress is the natural increase of population, which contributes more than any other influence to accelerate the speed. This increase has always been regarded as the clearest symptom of the gradual amelioration of the human condition; and nothing can be more unquestionable when we take the whole race into the account; or at least, all the nations which have any mutual interest: but this is not the view with which my argument is concerned. I have to consider only the progressive condensation of our species as a last general element concurring in the regulation of our rate of social progress. It is clear that by this condensation, and especially in its early stages, such a division of employments is favored as could not take place among smaller numbers: and again, that the faculties of individuals are stimulated to find subsistence by more refined methods: and again, that society is obliged to act with a firmer and better-concerted energy against the expansion of individual divergences. In view of these considerations, I speak, not of the increase of the numbers of mankind, but of their concentration upon a given space, according to the special expression which I have made use of, and which is particularly applicable to the great centres of population, whence, in all ages, human progression has started. By creating new wants and new difficulties, this gradual concentration develops new means, not only of progress but of order, by neutralizing physical inequalities, and affording a growing ascendency to those intellectual and moral forces which are suppressed among a scanty population. If we go on to inquire into the effect of a quicker or slower concentration, we shall perceive that the social movement is further accelerated by the disturbance given to the old antagonism between the conservative and the innovating instincts,—the last being strongly reinforced. In this sense, the sociological influence of a more rapid increase of population is in analogy with that which we have just been considering in regard to the duration of life; for it is of little consequence whether the more frequent renewal of individuals is caused by the short life of some, or the speedier multiplication of others; and what was said in the former case will suffice for the latter. It must be observed, however, that if the condensation and rapidity were to pass beyond a certain degree, they would not favor, but impede this acceleration. The condensation, if carried too far, would render the support of human life too difficult; and the rapidity, if extreme, would so affect the stability of social enterprises as to be equivalent to a considerable shortening of our life. As yet, however, the increase of population has never nearly reached the natural limits at which such inconveniences will begin; and we have really no experience of them, unless in a few exceptional cases of disturbance caused by migrations, ill-managed as to their extent of numbers and of time. In an extremely distant future, our posterity will have to consider the question, and with much anxiety; because, from the smallness of the globe, and the necessary limitation of human resources, the tendency to increase will become extremely important, when the human race will be ten times as numerous as at present, and as much condensed everywhere as it now is in the west of Europe. Whenever that time comes, the more complete development of human nature, and the more exact knowledge of the laws of human evolution, will no doubt supply new means of resistance to the danger; means of which we can form no clear conception, and about which it is not for us to decide whether they will, on the whole, afford a sufficient compensation.

These are not all the accelerating influences which could be mentioned; but they are the chief; and they are enough for us, in our abstract view of our subject. I have now only to exhibit the main subordination which the different aspects of human development must mutually present.

Though the elements of our social evolution are connected,

and always acting on each other, one must be preponderant, in order to give an impulse to the rest, though they may, in their turn, so act upon it as to cause its further expansion. We must find out this superior element, leaving the lower degrees of subordination to disclose themselves as we proceed: and we have not to search far for this element, as we can not err in taking that which can best be conceived of apart from the rest, notwithstanding their necessary connection, while the consideration of it would enter into the study of the others. This double characteristic points out the intellectual evolution as the preponderant principle. If the intellectual point of view was the chief in our statical study of the organism, much more must it be so in the dynamical case. If our reason required at the outset the awakening and stimulating influence of the appetites, the passions, and the sentiments, not the less has human progression gone forward under its direction. It is only through the more and more marked influence of the reason over the general conduct of Man and of society, that the gradual march of our race has attained that regularity and persevering continuity which distinguish it so radically from the desultory and barren expansion of even the highest of the animal orders, which share, and with enhanced strength, the appetites, the passions, and even the primary sentiments of Man. If the statical analysis of our social organism shows it resting at length upon a certain system of fundamental opinions, the gradual changes of that system must affect the successive modifications of the life of humanity: and this is why, since the birth of philosophy, the history of society has been regarded as governed by the history of the human mind. As it is necessary, in a scientific sense, to refer our historical analysis to the preponderant evolution, whatever it may be, we must in this case choose, or rather preserve, the general history of the human mind as the natural guide to all historical study of humanity. One consequence of the same principle—a consequence as rigorous but less understood—is that we must choose for consideration in this intellectual history, the most general and abstract conceptions, which require the exercise of our highest faculties. Thus it is the study of the fundamental system of human opinions with regard to the whole of phenomena—in short, the history of Philosophy, whatever may be its character, theological, metaphysical, or positive—which must regulate our historical analysis. No other department of intellectual history, not even the history of the fine arts, including poetry, could, however important in itself, be employed for this object; because the faculties of expression, which lie nearer to the affective faculties, have always, in their palmiest days, been subordinated, in the economy of social progress, to the faculties of direct conception. The danger (which is inherent in every choice, and which is the least in the choice that I have made) of losing sight of the interconnection of all the parts of human development, may be partly guarded against by frequently comparing them, to see if the variations in any one correspond with equivalent variations in the others. I believe we shall find that this confirmation is eminently obtainable by my method of historical analysis. This will be proved at once if we find that the development of the highest part of human interests is in accordance with that of the lowest—the intellectual with the material. If there is an accordance between the two extremes, there must be also between all the intermediate terms. . . .

The occasional rivalry between the theological power and the military, which history presents, has sometimes disguised their radical affinity, even in the eyes of philosophers. But, if we consider, there can be no real rivalry but among the different elements of the same political system, in consequence of that spontaneous emulation which, in all cases of human concurrence, must become more earnest and extensive as the end is more important and indirect, and therefore the means more distinct and independent, without the participation, voluntary or instinctive, being thereby prevented. When two powers, equally energetic, rise, increase, and decline together, notwithstanding the difference of their natures, we may be assured that they belong to the same régime, whatever may be their habitual conflicts. Conflict indicates radical incompatibility only when it takes place between two elements employed in analogous functions, and when the gradual growth of the one coincides with the continuous decline of the other. As to the present case, it is evident that, in any political system, there must be an incessant rivalry between the speculative and the active powers, which, through the imperfection of our nature, must often be inclined to ignore their necessary co-ordination, and to disdain the general limits of their reciprocal attributes. Notwithstanding the social affinity between science and industry, we must look for similar conflict between them hereafter, in proportion to the political ascendency which they will obtain together. We see signs of it already in the intellectual and moral antipathy of Science to the natural inferiority of these labors of Industry which yet are the means of wealth, and in the instinctive repugnance of Industry to the abstraction which characterizes Science, and to the just pride by which it is animated.

Having despatched these objections, we may now contemplate the strong bond which unites the theological and military powers, and which has in all ages been felt and honored by all enlightened men who have borne a part in either, notwithstanding the passions of political rivalry. It is plain that no military system could arise and endure without the countenance of the theological spirit, which must secure for it the complete and permanent subordination essential to its existence. Each period imposes equal exigences of this sort in its special manner. At the outset, when the narrowness and nearness of the aim required a less absolute submission of mind, social ties were so weak that nothing could have been done but for the religious authority with which military chiefs were naturally invested. In more advanced times the end became so vast and remote, and the participation so indirect, that even long habits of discipline would not have secured the necessary co-operation without the aid of theological convictions occasioning blind and involuntary confidence in military superiors. It was in very ancient times that the military spirit had its great social function to fulfil; and it was in those ancient times that the two powers were usually found concentred in the same chiefs. We must observe also that it was not every spiritual authority whatever that would have sufficiently suited the foundation and consolidation of military government, which, from its nature, required the concurrence of the theological philosophy, and no other: for instance, though natural philosophy has rendered eminent service in modern times to the art of war, the scientific spirit, which encourages habits of rational discussion, is radically incompatible with the military spirit; and we know that the subjection of their art to the principles of science has always been bitterly deplored by the most distinguished soldiers, on the introduction of every change, as a token of the decline of the military system. On this ground, then, the affinity of temporal military powers for spiritual theological powers is sufficiently accounted for. At the first glance we might suppose the converse relation to be less indispensable, since purely theocratic societies have existed, while an exclusively military one has never been known. But a closer examination will always show the necessity of the military system to consolidate, and yet more to extend, the theological authority, developed in this way by a continual political application, as the sacerdotal instinct has always been well aware. We shall see again that the theological spirit is as hostile to the expansion of industry as the military. Thus the two elements of the primitive political system have not only a radical affinity, but common antipathies and sympathies, as well as general interests; and it must be needless to enlarge further in this place on the sociological principle of the concurrence of these powers. . . .

The latest case of political dualism is even more unquestionable than the earliest, and we are favorably circumstanced for observing it —the two elements not having yet attained their definite ascendency, though their social development is sufficiently marked. When the time arrives for their political rivalry, it may be more difficult than now to exhibit that resemblance in origin and destination, and that conformity of principles and interests, which could not be seriously disputed as long as their common struggle against the old political system acts as a restraint upon their divergencies. The most remarkable feature that we have to contemplate in their case is the aid which each renders to the political triumph of the other, by seconding its own efforts against its chief antagonist. I have already noticed, in another connection, the secret incompatibility between the scientific spirit and the military. There is the same hostility between the industrial spirit, when sufficiently developed, and the theological. The most zealous advocates of the old *régime* are very far removed from the old religious point of view; but we can transport ourselves to it for a moment, and see how the voluntary modification of phenomena by the rules of human wisdom must thence appear as impious as the rational prevision of them, as both suppose invariable laws, finally irreconcilable with all arbitrary will. According to the rigorous though barbarous logic of the least-civilized nations, all human intervention to improve the economy of nature is an injurious attack upon providential government. There is no doubt, in fact, that a strong preponderance of the religious spirit benumbs the industrial, by the exaggerated feelings of a stupid optimism, as has been abundantly clear on many decisive occasions. That this disastrous effect has not been more fatal is owing to priestly sagacity, which has so managed this dangerous power as to educe its civilizing influence, while neutralizing its injurious action by constant and vigilant effort. . . . We can not, then, overlook the political influence by which the gradual expansion of human industry must aid the progressive ascendency of the scientific spirit, in its antagonism to the religious; to say nothing of the daily stimulus which industry and science impart to each other, when once strong enough for mutual action. Thus far their office has chiefly been to substitute themselves for the ancient political powers which are yielding up their social influence; and our attention is necessarily drawn chiefly to the aid they have afforded to each other in this operation. But it is easy to perceive what force and what efficacy must reside in their connection, when it shall have assumed the organic character, in which it is at present deficient, and shall proceed to the final reorganization of modern society.

Now that we have examined the two extreme states, the intermediate dualism requires little notice. The interconnection of the convergent powers, spiritual and temporal, which constitutes the transitory *régime*, is a necessary consequence of all that we have been observing. Indeed, we need but look at the labors of metaphysicians and legists to see what their affinity is, amidst their rivalries; an affinity which stakes the philosophical ascendency of the one class on the political preponderance of the other. We may, then, regard as now complete the necessary explanation required by our fundamental law of human evolution, in order to direct its application to the study of this great phenomenon. That study will be guided by the consideration of the three dualisms which I have established as the only basis of sound historical philosophy. It is worth noticing the conformity of this law of succession, at once intellectual and material, social and political, with the historical order which popular reason has instinctively established by distinguishing the ancient and the modern world, separated and reunited by the Middle Ages. The sociological law which I have propounded may be found to have for its destination to take up a vague empirical notion, hitherto barren, and render it rational and prolific. I hail this spontaneous coincidence, as giving a sanction to my speculative labors; and I claim this confirmation, in virtue of that great aphorism of positive philosophy which I have quoted so often, which enjoins upon all sound scientific theories to start from a point sufficiently accordant with the spontaneous indications of popular reason, of which true science is simply a special prolongation.

The series of views of social dynamics sketched out . . . has established the fundamental law of human development and therefore the bases of historical philosophy. . . .

12

Research Methods in Sociology

Comte places great emphasis upon observation as a part of sociological methods of investigation but he is emphatic in asserting that scientific observation was impossible unless it was used to test some law or theory concerning the behavior of phenomena. Anecdotal note-taking or surveying is not what he has in mind concerning observation. The validity of laws must be tested and, thus, sociology will come to consist in both its statical and dynamic parts of validated interconnections of social facts. Here he propounds the thesis: "No social fact can have any scientific meaning till it is connected with some other social fact."

Since sociological observation requires minds trained in theory, that know how to look and what to look for, sociology is no science for the poorly educated. Because social life hustles and bustles all about us does not mean that every man can make "positive" sense of its phenomena. But this hustle and bustle nevertheless offer the trained observer (that is, one educated in the sciences and in theoretical sociology) an embarrassment of riches. Data are literally there for the asking; the important thing is to see beyond the data and to be able to test and propound laws of social phenomena.

Comte's stress on sociological experiments was revolutionary when published in the Cours. He holds that if we cannot have "controlled" experiments, we are nevertheless offered a vast field where variables have been introduced that alter the course of social phenomena—pathological cases where disturbances occur in the social "organism." Indirect experimentation (indirect because the experimenter has not introduced the variables) will disclose the real workings of the social body in a more marked manner than simple observation could do. In other words, the study of pathology will lead us to laws of non-pathology, of co-existence of institutions

99

and evolutionary transitions. Comte notes that in his time experimentation has been little used but, once sociology develops ampli-
tude as a science, experimentation offers great possibilities for the
discovery of laws.

Comparison is crucial to Comte's methodology. That relating to
the "social" life of inferior animals will increase our understanding
of specifically human behavior and of human nature. The comparison of co-existing states of society in different parts of the globe
will help us to understand the aetiological factors which bring about
change as well as the uniformity of man in the midst of institutional
differences. Here Comte is offering a method which is today becoming highly significant in the comparison of so-called under-
developed and undeveloped societies with industrial societies. From
this comparison of co-existing states (statics), we are led to an understanding of the succession of social states, and, finally, to laws of general social evolution. This use of comparison was already made possible
by the theoretical law of the three stages or states. Thus, we are led
back to the necessity for a positive philosophy based on the unity
of science and its culmination in sociology.

Only as we discover through scientific methodology how and why
men live together as they have and as they do can we finally arrive
at an understanding of the morality befitting the present. And
so Comte's unity of thought inevitably leads him back to the question with which he first started his systematic thinking—by what
faith can men live in industrial society?

This adamant search for pertinent morality on Comte's part gives
sharp point to his having opened volume one of Positive Polity
with lines from the poet Alfred de Vigny: "What is a great life?
A thought of youth fulfilled in riper age."

1. Sociological Means of Investigation

. . . . The next step . . . is to examine . . . the means of investigation proper to Social Science. . . . We may expect to find in
Sociology a more varied and developed system of resources than
in any other, in proportion to the complexity of the phenomena,
while yet this extension of means does not compensate for the
increased imperfection arising from the intricacy. The extension of

SOURCE: Positive Philosophy, pp. 473–74.

the means is also more difficult to verify than in any prior case, from the novelty of the subject; and I can scarcely hope that such a sketch as I must present here will command such confidence as will arise when a complete survey of the science shall have confirmed what I now offer.

As Social Physics assumes a place in the hierarchy of sciences after all the rest and therefore dependent on them, its means of investigation must be of two kinds: those which arise from the connection of sociology with the other sciences; and these last, though indirect, are as indispensable as the first. I shall review . . . the direct resources of the science.

2. Observation

Very imperfect and even vicious notions prevail at present as to what Observation can be and can effect in Social Science. The chaotic state of doctrine of the last century has extended to Method; and amidst our intellectual disorganization, difficulties have been magnified; precautionary methods, experimental and rational, have been broken up; and even the possibility of obtaining social knowledge by observation has been dogmatically denied; but if the sophisms put forth on this subject were true, they would destroy the certainty, not only of social science, but of all the simpler and more perfect ones that have gone before. The ground of doubt assigned is the uncertainty of human testimony; but all the sciences, up to the most simple, require proofs of testimony: that is, in the elaboration of the most positive theories, we have to admit observations which could not be directly made, nor even repeated, by those who use them, and the reality of which rests only on the faithful testimony of the original investigators; there being nothing in this to prevent the use of such proofs, in concurrence with immediate observations. In Astronomy, such a method is obviously necessary; it is equally, though less obviously, necessary even in mathematics; and, of course, much more evidently in the case of the more complex sciences. How could any science emerge from the nascent state—how could there be any organization of intellectual labor, even if research were restricted to the utmost, if every one rejected all observations but his own? The stoutest advocates

SOURCE: *Positive Philosophy*, pp. 474–77.

of historical skepticism do not go so far as to advocate this. It is only in the case of social phenomena that the paradox is proposed; and it is made use of there because it is one of the weapons of the philosophical arsenal which the revolutionary metaphysical doctrine constructed for the intellectual overthrow of the ancient political system. The next great hindrance to the use of observation is the empiricism which is introduced into it by those who, in the name of impartiality, would interdict the use of any theory whatever. No logical dogma could be more thoroughly irreconcilable with the spirit of the positive philosophy, or with its special character in regard to the study of social phenomena, than this. No real observation of any kind of phenomena is possible, except in as far as it is first directed, and finally interpreted, by some theory: and it was this logical need which, in the infancy of human reason, occasioned the rise of theological philosophy, as we shall see in the course of our historical survey. The positive philosophy does not dissolve this obligation, but, on the contrary, extends and fulfils it more and more, the further the relations of phenomena are multiplied and perfected by it. Hence it is clear that, scientifically speaking, all isolated, empirical observation is idle, and even radically uncertain; that science can use only those observations which are connected, at least hypothetically, with some law; that it is such a connection which makes the chief difference between scientific and popular observation, embracing the same facts, but contemplating them from different points of view: and that observations empirically conducted can at most supply provisional materials, which must usually undergo an ulterior revision. The rational method of observation becomes more necessary in proportion to the complexity of the phenomena, amid which the observer would not know what he ought to look at in the facts before his eyes, but for the guidance of a preparatory theory; and thus it is that by the connection of foregoing facts we learn to see the facts that follow. This is undisputed with regard to astronomical, physical, and chemical research, and in every branch of biological study, in which good observation of its highly complex phenomena is still very rare, precisely because its positive theories are very imperfect. Carrying on the analogy, it is evident that in the corresponding divisions, statical and dynamical, of social science, there is more need than anywhere else of theories which shall scientifically connect the facts that are happening with those that have happened: and the more we reflect, the more distinctly we shall see that in proportion as known facts are mutually connected we shall be better able, not only to estimate, but to perceive, those which are yet unexplored. I am not blind to the vast difficulty which this requisition imposes on the institution of positive sociology—obliging us to create at once, so to speak, observations and laws, on account of their indispensable connection, placing us in a sort of vicious circle, from which we can issue only by employing in the first instance materials which are badly elaborated, and doctrines which are ill-conceived. How I may succeed in a task so difficult and delicate, we shall see . . . ; but, however that may be, it is clear that it is the absence of any positive theory which at present renders social observations so vague and incoherent. There can never be any lack of facts; for in this case even more than in others, it is the commonest sort of facts that are most important, whatever the collectors of secret anecdotes may think; but, though we are steeped to the lips in them, we can make no use of them, nor even be aware of them, for want of speculative guidance in examining them. The statical observation of a crowd of phenomena can not take place without some notion, however elementary, of the laws of social interconnection: and dynamical facts could have no fixed direction if they were not attached, at least by a provisional hypothesis, to the laws of social development. The positive philosophy is very far from discouraging historical or any other erudition; but the precious night-watchings, now so lost in the laborious acquisition of a conscientious but barren learning, may be made available by it for the constitution of true social science, and the increased honor of the earnest minds that are devoted to it. The new philosophy will supply fresh and nobler subjects, unhoped-for insight, a loftier aim, and therefore a higher scientific dignity. It will discard none but aimless labors, without principle and without character; as in Physics, there is no room for compilations of empirical observations; and at the same time, philosophy will render justice to the zeal of students of a past generation, who, destitute of the favorable guidance which we, of this day, enjoy, followed up their laborious historical researches with an instinctive perseverance, and in spite of the superficial disdain of the philosophers of the time. No doubt, the same danger attends research here as elsewhere: the danger that, from the continuous use of scientific theories, the observer may sometimes pervert facts, by erroneously supposing them to verify some ill-grounded speculative prejudices of his own. But we have the same guard here as elsewhere—in the further extension of the science: and the case would

not be improved by a recurrence to empirical methods, which
would be merely leaving theories that may be misapplied but can
always be rectified, for imaginary notions which can not be substan
tiated at all. Our feeble reason may often fail in the application
of positive theories; but at least they transfer us from the domain
of imagination to that of reality, and expose us infinitely less than
any other kind of doctrine to the danger of seeing in facts that
which is not.

It is now clear that Social Science requires, more than any other
the subordination of Observation to the statical and dynamical law
of phenomena. No social fact can have any scientific meaning till
it is connected with some other social fact; without which connec
tion it remains a mere anecdote, involving no rational utility. This
condition so far increases the immediate difficulty that good ob
servers will be rare at first, though more abundant than ever as the
science expands: and here we meet with another confirmation of
what I said at the outset . . . —that the formation of social theorie
should be confided only to the best organized minds, prepared by
the most rational training. Explored by such minds, according to
rational views of co-existence and succession, social phenomena no
doubt admit of much more varied and extensive means of investiga
tion than phenomena of less complexity. In this view, it is not only
the immediate inspection or direct description of events that afford
useful means of positive exploration; but the consideration of ap
parently insignificant customs, the appreciation of various kind
of monuments, the analysis and comparison of languages, and a
multitude of other resources. In short, a mind suitably trained be
comes able by exercise to convert almost all impressions from the
events of life into sociological indications, when once the connection
of all indications with the leading ideas of the science is under
stood. This is a facility afforded by the mutual relation of the various
aspects of society, which may partly compensate for the difficulty
caused by that mutual connection: if it renders observation more
difficult, it affords more means for its prosecution.

3. Experiment

It might be supposed beforehand that the second method of investigation, Experiment, must be wholly inapplicable in Social Science; but we shall find that the science is not entirely deprived of this resource, though it must be one of inferior value. We must remember . . . that there are two kinds of experimentation—the direct and the indirect: and that it is not necessary to the philosophical character of this method that the circumstances of the phenomenon in question should be, as is vulgarly supposed in the learned world, artificially instituted. Whether the case be natural or factitious, experimentation takes place whenever the regular course of the phenomenon is interfered with in any determinate manner. The spontaneous nature of the alteration has no effect on the scientific value of the case, if the elements are known. It is in this sense that experimentation is possible in Sociology. If direct experimentation had become too difficult amidst the complexities of biology, it may well be considered impossible in Social Science. Any artificial disturbance of any social element must affect all the rest, according to the laws both of co-existence and succession; and the experiment would therefore, if it could be instituted at all, be deprived of all scientific value, through the impossibility of isolating either the conditions or the results of the phenomenon. But we saw . . . that pathological cases are the true scientific equivalent of pure experimentation, and why. The same reasons apply, with even more force, to sociological researches. In them, pathological analysis consists in the examination of cases, unhappily too common, in which the natural laws, either of harmony or of succession, are disturbed by any causes, special or general, accidental or transient; as in revolutionary times especially; and above all, in our own. These disturbances are, in the social body, exactly analogous to diseases in the individual organism: and I have no doubt whatever that the analogy will be more evident (allowance being made for the unequal complexity of the organisms) the deeper the investigation goes. In both cases it is . . . a noble use to make of our reason, to disclose the real laws of our nature, individual or social, by the analysis of its sufferings. But if the method is imperfectly

SOURCE: *Positive Philosophy*, pp. 477–78.

instituted in regard to biological questions, much more faulty must it be in regard to the phenomena of Social Science, for want even of the rational conceptions to which they are to be referred. We see the most disastrous political experiments for ever renewed, with only some insignificant and irrational modifications, though their first operation should have fully satisfied us of the uselessness and danger of the expedients proposed. Without forgetting how much is ascribable to the influence of human passions, we must remember that the deficiency of an authoritative rational analysis is one of the main causes of the barrenness imputed to social experiments, the course of which would become much more instructive if it were better observed. The great natural laws exist and act in all conditions of the organism; for as . . . in the case of biology, it is an error to suppose that they are violated or suspended in the case of disease: and we are therefore justified in drawing our conclusions, with due caution, from the scientific analysis of disturbance to the positive theory of normal existence. This is the nature and character of the indirect experimentation which discloses the real economy of the social body in a more marked manner than simple observation could do. It is applicable to all orders of sociological research, whether relating to existence or to movement, and regarded under any aspect whatever, physical, intellectual, moral or political; and to all degrees of the social evolution, from which, unhappily, disturbances have never been absent. As for its present extension, no one can venture to offer any statement of it, because it has never been duly applied in any investigation in political philosophy; and it can become customary only by the institution of the new science which I am endeavoring to establish. But I could not omit this notice of it, as one of the means of investigation proper to social science.

4. Comparison

As for the third of those methods, Comparison, the reader must bear in mind the explanations offered, in our survey of biological philosophy, of the reasons why the comparative method must prevail in all studies of which the living organism is the subject; and the more remarkably, in proportion to the rank of the organism. The same considerations apply in the present case, in a more conspicuous

SOURCE: *Positive Philosophy*, pp. 478–85.

degree; and I may leave it to the reader to make the application, merely pointing out the chief differences which distinguish the use of the comparative method in sociological inquiries.

It is a very irrational disdain which makes us object to all comparison between human society and the social state of the lower animals. This unphilosophical pride arose out of the protracted influence of the theologico-metaphysical philosophy; and it will be corrected by the positive philosophy, when we better understand and can estimate the social state of the higher orders of mammifers, for instance. We have seen how important is the study of individual life, in regard to intellectual and moral phenomena—of which social phenomena are the natural result and complement. There was once the same blindness to the importance of the procedure in this case as now in the other; and as it has given way in the one case, so it will in the other. The chief defect in the kind of sociological comparison that we want is that it is limited to statical considerations; whereas the dynamical are, at the present time, the preponderant and direct subject of science. The restriction results from the social state of animals being, though not so stationary as we are apt to suppose, yet susceptible only of extremely small variations, in no way comparable to the continued progression of humanity in its feeblest days. But there is no doubt of the scientific utility of such a comparison, in the statical province, where it characterizes the elementary laws of social interconnection, by exhibiting their action in the most imperfect state of society, so as even to suggest useful inductions in regard to human society. There can not be a stronger evidence of the natural character of the chief social relations, which some people fancy that they can transform at pleasure. Such sophists will cease to regard the great ties of the human family as factitious and arbitrary when they find them existing, with the same essential characteristics, among the animals, and more conspicuously, the nearer the organisms approach to the human type. In brief, in all that part of sociology which is almost one with intellectual and moral biology, or with the natural history of Man; in all that relates to the first germs of the social relations, and the first institutions which were founded by the unity of the family or the tribe, there is not only great scientific advantage, but real philosophical necessity for employing the rational comparison of human with other animal societies. Perhaps it might even be desirable not to confine the comparison to societies which present a character of voluntary cooperation, in analogy to the human. They must always rank first in importance: but the scientific spirit, extending the process to its final logical term, might find some advantage in examining those strange associations, proper to the inferior animals, in which an involuntary co-operation results from an indissoluble organic union, either by simple adhesion or real continuity. If the science gained nothing by this extension, the method would. And there is nothing that can compare with such an habitual scientific comparison for the great service of casting out the absolute spirit which is the chief vice of political philosophy. It appears to me, moreover, that, in a practical view, the insolent pride which induces some ranks of society to suppose themselves as, in a manner, of another species than the rest of mankind, is in close affinity with the irrational disdain that repudiates all comparison between human and other animal nature. However all this may be, these considerations apply only to a methodical and special treatment of social philosophy. Here, where I can offer only the first conception of the science, in which dynamical considerations must prevail, it is evident that I can make little use of the kind of comparison; and this makes it all the more necessary to point it out, lest its omission should occasion such scientific inconveniences as I have just indicated. The commonest logical procedures are generally so characterized by their very application, that nothing more of a preliminary nature is needed than the simplest examination of their fundamental properties.

To indicate the order of importance of the forms of society which are to be studied by the Comparative Method, I begin with the chief method, which consists in a comparison of the different coexisting states of human society on the various parts of the earth's surface— those states being completely independent of each other. By this method, the different stages of evolution may all be observed at once. Though the progression is single and uniform, in regard to the whole race, some very considerable and very various populations have, from causes which are little understood, attained extremely unequal degrees of development, so that the former states of the most civilized nations are now to be seen, amid some partial differences, among contemporary populations inhabiting different parts of the globe. In its relation to Observation, this kind of comparison offers the advantage of being applicable both to statical and dynamical inquiries, verifying the laws of both, and even furnishing occasionally valuable direct inductions in regard to both. In the second place, it exhibits all possible degrees of social evolution to our immediate observation. From the wretched inhabitants of Tierra del Fuego to the most advanced nations of western Europe, there is no social grade which is not extant in some points of the globe, and usually in localities which are clearly apart. We shall find that some interesting secondary phases of social development, of which the history of civilization leaves no perceptible traces, can be known only by this comparative method of study; and these are not, as might be supposed, the lowest degrees of evolution, which every one admits can be investigated in no other way. And between the great historical aspects, there are numerous intermediate states which must be observed thus, if at all. This second part of the comparative method verifies the indications afforded by historical analysis, and fills up the gaps it leaves: and nothing can be more rational than the method, as it rests upon the established principle that the development of the human mind is uniform in the midst of all diversities of climate, and even of race; such diversities having no effect upon anything more than the rate of progress. But we must beware of the scientific dangers attending the process of comparison by this method. For instance, it can give us no idea of the order of succession, as it presents all the states of development as coexisting: so that, if the order of development were not established by other methods, this one would infallibly mislead us. And again, if we were not misled as to the order, there is nothing in this method which discloses the filiation of the different systems of society; a matter in which the most distinguished philosophers have been mistaken in various ways and degrees. Again, there is the danger of mistaking modifications for primary phases; as when social differences have been ascribed to the political influence of climate, instead of that inequality of evolution which is the real cause. Sometimes, but more rarely, the mistake is the other way. Indeed, there is nothing in the matter that can show which of two cases presents the diversity that is observed. We are in danger of the same mistake in regard to races; for, as the sociological comparison is instituted between peoples of different races, we are liable to confound the effects of race and of the social period. Again, climate comes in to offer a third source of interpretation of comparative phenomena, sometimes agreeing with, and sometimes contradicting the two others; thus multiplying the chances of error, and rendering the analysis which looked so promising almost impracticable. Here, again, we see the indispensable necessity of keeping in view the positive conception of human development as a whole. By this alone can we be preserved from such errors as I have referred to, and enriched by any genuine results of analysis. We see how absurd in theory and dangerous in practice are the notions and declamations of the empirical school, and of the enemies of all social speculation: for it is precisely in proportion to their elevation and generality that the ideas of positive social philosophy become real and effective—an illusion and uselessness belonging to conceptions which are too narrow and too special, in the departments either of science or of reasoning. But it is a consequence from these last considerations that this first sketch of sociological science, with the means of investigation that belong to it, rests immediately upon the primary use of a new method of observation, which is so appropriate to the nature of the phenomena as to be exempt from the dangers inherent in the others. This last portion of the comparative method is the Historical Method, properly so called; and it is the only basis on which the system of political logic can rest.

The historical comparison of the consecutive states of humanity is not only the chief scientific device of the new political philosophy. Its rational development constitutes the substratum of the science, in whatever is essential to it. It is this which distinguishes it thoroughly from biological science. . . . The positive principle of this separation results from the necessary influence of human generations upon the generations that follow, accumulating continuously till it constitutes the preponderating consideration in the direct study of social development. As long as this preponderance is not directly recognised, the positive study of humanity must appear a simple prolongation of the natural history of Man: but this scientific character, suitable enough to the earlier generations, disappears in the course of the social evolution, and assumes at length a wholly new aspect, proper to sociological science, in which historical considerations are of immediate importance. And this preponderant use of the historical method gives its philosophical character to sociology in a logical as well as a scientific sense. By the creation of this new department of the comparative method, sociology confers a benefit on the whole of natural philosophy; because the positive method is thus completed and perfected, in a manner which, for scientific importance, is almost beyond our estimate. What we can now comprehend is that the historical method verifies and applies, in the largest way, that chief quality of sociological science—its proceeding from the whole to the parts. Without this permanent condition of social study, all historical labor would degenerate into being a mere compilation of provisional materials. As it is in their development, especially, that the various social elements are interconnected and inseparable, it is clear that any partial filiation must be essentially untrue. Where, for instance, is the use of any exclusive history of any one science or art, unless meaning is given to it by first connecting it with the study of human progress generally? It is the same in every direction, and especially with regard to political history, as it is called; as if any history could be other than political, more or less! The prevailing tendency to speciality in study would reduce history to a mere accumulation of unconnected delineations, in which all idea of the true filiation of events would be lost amid the mass of confused descriptions. If the historical comparisons of the different periods of civilization are to have any scientific character, they must be referred to the general social evolution: and it is only thus that we can obtain the guiding ideas by which the special studies themselves must be directed.

In a practical view, it is evident that the preponderance of the historical method tends to develop the social sentiment, by giving us an immediate interest in even the earliest experiences of our race, through the influence that they exercised over the evolution of our own civilization. As Condorcet observed, no enlightened man can think of the battles of Marathon and Salamis without perceiving the importance of their consequences to the race at large. This kind of feeling should, when we are treating of science, be carefully distinguished from the sympathetic interest which is awakened by all delineations of human life—in fiction as well as in history. The sentiment I refer to is deeper, because in some sort personal; and more reflective, because it results from scientific conviction. It can not be excited by popular history in a descriptive form; but only by positive history, regarded as a true science, and exhibiting the events of human experience in co-ordinated series which manifest their own graduated connection. This new form of the social sentiment must at first be the privilege of the choice few; but it will be extended, somewhat weakened in force, to the whole of society, in proportion as the general results of social physics become sufficiently popular. It will fulfil the most obvious and elementary idea of the habitual connection between individuals and contemporary nations, by showing that the successive generations of men concur in a final end, which requires the determinate participation of each and all. This rational disposition to regard men of all times as fellow-workers is as yet visible in the case of only the most advanced sciences. By the philosophical preponderance of the historical method, it will be extended to all the aspects of human life, so as to sustain, in a reflective temper, that respect for our ancestors which is indispensable to a sound state of society, and so deeply disturbed at present by the metaphysical philosophy.

As for the course to be pursued by this method—it appears to me that its spirit consists in the rational use of social series; that is, in a successive estimate of the different states of humanity which shall show the growth of each disposition, physical, intellectual, moral, or political, combined with the decline of the opposite disposition, whence we may obtain a scientific prevision of the final ascendency of the one and extinction of the other—care being taken to frame our conclusions according to the laws of human development. A considerable accuracy of prevision may thus be obtained, for any determinate period, and with any particular view; as historical analysis will indicate the direction of modifications, even in the most disturbed times. And it is worth noticing that the prevision will be nearest the truth in proportion as the phenomena in question are more important and more general; because then continuous causes are predominant in the social movement; and disturbances have less power. From these first general aspects, the same rational certainty may extend to secondary and special aspects, through their statical relations with the first; and thus we may obtain conclusions sufficiently accurate for the application of principles.

If we desire to familiarize ourselves with this historical method, we must employ it first upon the past, by endeavoring to deduce every well-known historical situation from the whole series of its antecedents. In every science we must have learned to predict the past, so to speak, before we can predict the future; because the first use of the observed relations among fulfilled facts is to teach us by the anterior succession what the future succession will be. No examination of facts can explain our existing state to us, if we have not ascertained, by historical study, the value of the elements at work; and thus it is in vain that statesmen insist on the necessity of political observation, while they look no further than the present, or a very recent past. The present is, by itself, purely misleading, because it is impossible to avoid confounding principal with secondary facts, exalting conspicuous transient manifestations over fundamental tendencies, which are generally very quiet; and above all, supposing those powers, institutions, and doctrines, to be in the ascendant, which are, in fact, in their decline. It is clear that the only adequate corrective of all this is a philosophical understanding of the past; that the comparison can not be decisive unless it embraces the whole of the past; and that the sooner we stop, in travelling up the vista of time, the more serious will be the mistakes we fall into. Before our very eyes, we see statesmen going no farther back than the last century, to obtain an explanation of the confusion in which we are living: the most abstract of politicians may take in the preceding century, but the philosophers themselves hardly venture beyond the sixteenth; so that those who are striving to find the issue of the revolutionary period have actually no conception of it as a whole, though that whole is itself only a transient phase of the general social movement.

The most perfect methods may, however, be rendered deceptive by misuse: and this we must bear in mind. We have seen that mathematical analysis itself may betray us into substituting signs for ideas, and that it conceals inanity of conception under an imposing verbiage. The difficulty in the case of the historical method in sociology is in applying it, on account of the extreme complexity of the materials we have to deal with. But for this, the method would be entirely safe. The chief danger is of our supposing a continuous decrease to indicate a final extinction, or the reverse; as in mathematics it is a common sophism to confound continuous variations, more or less, with unlimited variations. To take a strange and very marked example: if we consider that part of social development which relates to human food, we can not but observe that men take less food as they advance in civilization. If we compare savage with more civilized peoples, in the Homeric poems or in the narratives of travellers, or compare country with town life, or any generation with the one that went before, we shall find this curious result. . . . The laws of individual human nature aid in the result by making intellectual and moral action more preponderant as Man becomes more civilized. The fact is thus established, both by the experimental and the logical way. Yet nobody supposes that men will ultimately cease to eat. In this case, the absurdity saves us from a false conclusion; but in other cases, the complexity disguises much error in the experiment and the reasoning. In the above instance, we must resort to the laws of our nature for that verification which, taken all together, they afford to our sociological analysis. As the social phenomenon, taken as a whole, is simply a development of humanity, without any real creation of faculties, all social manifestations must be found, if only in their germ, in the primitive type which biology constructed by anticipation for sociology. Thus every law of social succession disclosed by the historical method must be unquestionably connected, directly or indirectly, with the positive theory of human nature; and all inductions which can not stand this test will prove to be illusory, through some sort of insufficiency in the observations on which they are grounded. The main scientific strength of sociological demonstrations must ever lie in the accordance between the conclusions of historical analysis and the preparatory conceptions of the biological theory. And thus we find, look where we will, a confirmation of that chief intellectual character of the new science— the philosophical preponderance of the spirit of the whole over the spirit of detail.

This method ranks, in sociological science, with that of zoological comparison in the study of individual life; . . . the succession of social states exactly corresponds, in a scientific sense, with the gradation of organisms in biology; and the social series, once clearly established, must be as real and as useful as the animal series. When the method has been used long enough to disclose its properties, I am disposed to think that it will be regarded as so very marked a modification of positive research as to deserve a separate place; so that, in addition to Observation, properly so called, Experiment, and Comparison, we shall have the Historical Method, as a fourth and final mode of the art of observing. It will be derived, according to the usual course, from the mode which immediately precedes it: and it will be applied to the analysis of the most complex phenomena.

I must be allowed to point out that the new political philosophy, sanctioning the old leadings of popular reason, restores to History all its scientific rights as a basis of wise social speculation, after the metaphysical philosophy had striven to induce us to discard all large consideration of the past. In the foregoing departments of natural philosophy we have seen that the positive spirit, instead of being disturbing in its tendencies, is remarkable for confirming, in the essential parts of every science, the inestimable intuitions of popular good sense; of which indeed science is merely a systematic prolongation, and which a barren metaphysical philosophy alone could despise. In this case, so far from restricting the influence which human reason has ever attributed to history in political combinations, the new social philosophy increases it, radically and eminently. It asks from history something more than counsel and instruction to perfect conceptions which are derived from another source: it seeks its own general direction, through the whole system of historical conclusions.

13

The Sociology of Knowledge
and of Science

It is clearly confirmed that Auguste Comte has been unjustifiably neglected in contemporary sociology when it is realized that almost no attention has been paid to him in the field known prestigiously as the sociology of knowledge (and of science) which deals with the socio-cultural factors associated with thought and its various forms of expression. A few pertinent lines are to be found in Raymond Aron's Main Currents in Sociological Thought (volume one):

. . . Sociology, for Comte, is the science of the human mind. Man understands the human mind only on condition that he observe its activity and its productions throughout history and in society. One does not come to know the human mind either through introspection, in the manner of the psychologists, or by the method of reflexive analysis, in the manner of Kant. The true science of the human mind is what we would today call the sociology of knowledge. The true science of the human mind is the observation, analysis, and comprehension of the capacities of the human mind as they are revealed to us through their productions in the course of history. Sociology is also the science of the human mind, because the mind's way of thinking and activity are at every moment inseparable from the social context. There is no transcendental, timeless self which can be grasped by means of reflexive analysis. The mind is social; it is historical: the mind of each age, the mind of each thinker, is caught in a social context.

In both the Cours and Politique positive we find analyses that show Comte to be preeminently a sociologist of knowledge. Indeed, the growth of positivism itself is determined by, conditioned by, or dependent upon social factors that promote the advancement of knowledge. The earlier stages of social development (theological and metaphysical) made only certain kinds of knowledge possible, and to a limited extent. Positivism opens the doors to the expansion of all knowledge by showing its social roots. In so far as earlier forms of knowledge were pregnant with sociological insights and understanding, they forged ahead. They fell back or languished as this sociological content became either retrograde or negative.

In order to pursue science, men must be organized in professional groups. This organization is determined by the existing state of social institutions (statics) and the dynamism for change they permit. The present bureaucratic state of science with its anomic and overrefined division of labor is a direct reflection of the bureaucratization of social life in general and of the lack of social principles needed to coordinate and guide human behavior. As each science enlarges as a sociological phenomenon it becomes, as a whole or in part, a factor in its own further development.

The laws of the mind, as discovered by sociology, determine the very future of science. Thus, sociology finally comes to direct the pursuit of scientific knowledge and man's social abilities determine what can be discovered. "Man is the measure of all things" is translated as "Man is the determiner of all scientific principles." Intellectual unity is afforded by sociology. The advancement of the inorganic and organic sciences is made possible by this intellectual unity and the positivist "state" of mind determines the philosophical validity of the abstractions of science.

It is not only scientific knowledge which is socially determined. As Berger and Luckman show, the sociology of knowledge also deals with what every man knows or thinks he knows. This area of public knowledge is also determined by social factors—preeminently education and communication. Positivism (consisting of the philosophical unity of knowledge) proclaims what every man should know and establishes the moral principles by which he can learn to use such knowledge to guide his behavior. Sociology establishes the future course of society by showing how this knowledge should be utilized or is being utilized.

1. *Humanity: The Basis of All Science*

. . . The Universe is to be studied not for its own sake, but for the sake of Man or rather of Humanity. To study it in any other spirit would not only be immoral, but also highly irrational. For, as statements of pure objective truth, our scientific theories can never be really satisfactory. They can only satisfy us from the subjective point of view; that is, by limiting themselves to the treatment of such questions as have some direct or indirect influence over human life. It is for social feeling to determine these limits; outside which our knowledge will always remain imperfect as well as useless, and this even in the case of the simplest phenomena, as astronomy testifies. Were the influence of social feeling to be slackened, the Positive spirit would soon fall back to the subjects which were preferred during the period of its infancy; subjects the most remote from human interests, and therefore also the easiest. While its probationary period lasted, it was natural to investigate all accessible problems without distinction; and this was often justified by the logical value of many problems that, scientifically speaking, were useless. But now that the Positive method has been sufficiently developed to be applied exclusively to the purpose for which it was intended, there is no use whatever in prolonging the period of probation by these idle exercises. Indeed the want of purpose and discipline in our researches is rapidly assuming a retrograde character. Its tendency is to undo the chief results obtained by the spirit of detail during the time when that spirit was really essential to progress. . . .

The fact of entire freedom from theological belief being necessary before the Positive state can be perfectly attained has induced superficial observers to confound Positivism with a state of pure negation. Now this state was at one time, and that even so recently as the last century, favourable to progress; but at present in those who unfortunately still remain in it, it is a radical obstacle to all sound social and even intellectual organisation. I have long ago repudiated all philosophical or historical connection between Positivism and what is called Atheism. But it is desirable to expose the error somewhat more clearly.

Atheism, even from the intellectual point of view, is a very imperfect form of emancipation; for its tendency is to prolong the

SOURCE: *Positive Polity*, Vol. I, pp. 28, 36–44, 46.

metaphysical stage indefinitely, by continuing to seek for new solutions of Theological problems, instead of setting aside all inaccessible researches on the ground of their utter inutility. The true Positive spirit consists in substituting the study of the invariable Laws of phenomena, for that of their so-called Causes, whether proximate or primary; in a word, in studying the How instead of the Why. Now, this is wholly incompatible with the ambitious and visionary attempts of Atheism to explain the formation of the Universe, the origin of animal life, etc. The Positivist, comparing the various phases of human speculation, looks upon these scientific chimeras as far less valuable even from the intellectual point of view than the first spontaneous inspirations of primeval times. The principle of Theology is to explain everything by supernatural Wills. That principle can never be set aside until we acknowledge the search for Causes to be beyond our reach, and limit ourselves to the knowledge of Laws. As long as men persist in attempting to answer the insoluble questions which occupied the attention of the childhood of our race, by far the more rational plan is, to do as was done then, that is, simply to give free play to the imagination. These spontaneous beliefs have gradually fallen into disuse, not because they have been disproved, but because mankind has become more enlightened as to its wants and the scope of its powers, and has gradually given an entirely new direction to its speculative efforts. If we insist upon penetrating the unattainable mystery of the essential Cause that produces phenomena, there is no hypothesis more satisfactory than that they proceed from Wills dwelling in them or outside them: an hypothesis which assimilates them to the effect produced by the desires which exist within ourselves. Were it not for the pride induced by metaphysical and scientific studies, it would be inconceivable that any Atheist, modern or ancient, should have believed that his vague hypotheses on such a subject were preferable to this direct mode of explanation. And it was the only mode which really satisfied the reason, until men began to see the utter inanity and inutility of all search for absolute truth. The Order of Nature is doubtless very imperfect in every respect; but its production would be far more compatible with the hypothesis of an intelligent Will than with that of a blind mechanism. Persistent Atheists, therefore, would seem to be the most illogical of theologists; because they occupy themselves with theological problems, and yet reject the only appropriate method of handling them. But the fact is, that pure Atheism even in the present day is very rare. What is called Atheism is usually a phase of Pantheism, which is really nothing but a relapse disguised under learned terms into a vague and abstract form of Fetichism. And it is not impossible that it may lead to the reproduction in one form or other of every theological phase, as soon as the check which modern society still imposes on metaphysical extravagance has become somewhat weakened. The adoption of such theories as a satisfactory system of belief indicates a very exaggerated or rather false view of intellectual requirements, and a very insufficient recognition of moral and social wants. It is generally connected with the visionary but mischievous tendencies of ambitious thinkers to uphold what they call the empire of Reason. In the moral sphere, it forms a sort of basis for the degrading fallacies of modern metaphysicians as to the absolute preponderance of self-interest. Politically, its tendency is to unlimited prolongation of the revolutionary position: its spirit is that of blind hatred to the past; and it resists all attempts to explain it on Positive principles, with the view of disclosing the future. Atheism, therefore, is not likely to lead to Positivism except in those who pass through it rapidly as the last and most short-lived of metaphysical phases. And the wide diffusion of the scientific spirit in the present day makes this passage so easy that to arrive at maturity without accomplishing it is a symptom of a certain mental weakness, which is often connected with moral insufficiency, and is very incompatible with Positivism. Negation offers but a feeble and precarious basis for union: and disbelief in Monotheism is of itself no better proof of a mind fit to grapple with the questions of the day than disbelief in Polytheism or Fetichism, which no one would maintain to be an adequate ground for claiming intellectual sympathy. The Atheistic phase indeed was not really necessary, except for the revolutionists of the last century who took the lead in the movement towards radical regeneration of society. The necessity has already ceased; for the decayed condition of the old system makes the need of regeneration palpable to all. Persistency in anarchy, and Atheism is the most characteristic symptom of anarchy, is a temper of mind more unfavourable to the organic spirit, which ought by this time to have established its influence, than sincere adhesion to the old forms. This latter is of course obstructive: but at least it does not hinder us from fixing our attention upon the great social problem. Indeed it helps us to do so; because it forces the new philosophy to throw aside every weapon of attack against the older faith except its own higher capacity of satisfying our moral and social wants. But from the Atheism maintained by many metaphysicians and scientific men of the present day, Positivism, instead of wholesome rivalry of this kind, will meet with nothing but barren resistance. Anti-theological as such men may be, they feel unmixed repugnance for any attempts at social regeneration, although their efforts in the last century had to some extent prepared the way for it. Far then, from counting upon their support, Positivists must expect to find them hostile: although from the incoherence of their opinions it will not be difficult to reclaim those of them whose errors are not essentially due to pride.

The charge of Materialism which is often made against Positive philosophy is of more importance. It originates in the course of scientific study upon which the Positive System is based. In answering the charge, I need not enter into any discussion of impenetrable mysteries. Our theory of development will enable us to see distinctly the real ground of the confusion that exists upon the subject.

Positive science was for a long time limited to the simplest subjects; it could not reach the highest except by a natural series of intermediate steps. As each of these steps is taken, the student is apt to be influenced too strongly by the methods and results of the preceding stage. Here, as it seems to me, lies the real source of that scientific error which men have instinctively blamed as Materialism. The name is just, because the tendency indicated is one which degrades the higher subjects of thought by confounding them with the lower. It was hardly possible that this usurpation by one science of the domain of another should have been wholly avoided. For since the more special phenomena do really depend upon the more general, it is perfectly legitimate for each science to exercise a certain deductive influence upon that which follows it in the scale. By such influence the special inductions of that science were rendered more coherent. The result, however, is that each of the sciences has to undergo a long struggle against the encroachments of the one preceding it; a struggle which, even in the case of the subjects which have been studied longest, is not yet over. Nor can it entirely cease until the controlling influence of sound philosophy be established over the whole scale, introducing juster views of the relations of its several parts, about which at present there is such irrational confusion. Thus it appears that Materialism is a danger inherent in the mode in which the scientific studies necessary as a preparation for Positivism were pursued. Each science tended to absorb the one next to it, on the ground of having reached the Positive stage earlier and more thoroughly. The evil then is really deeper and more extensive than is imagined by most of those who deplore it. It passes generally unnoticed except in the highest class of subjects. These doubtless are more seriously affected, inasmuch as they undergo the encroaching process from all the rest; but we find the same thing in different degrees, in every step of the scientific scale. Even the lowest step, Mathematics, is no exception, though its position would seem at first sight to exempt it. To a philosophic eye there is Materialism in the common tendency of mathematicians at the present day to absorb Geometry or Mechanics into the Calculus, as well as in the more evident encroachments of Mathematics upon Physics, of Physics upon Chemistry, of Chemistry, which is more frequent, upon Biology, or lastly in the common tendency of the best biologists to look upon Sociology as a mere corollary of their own science. In all these cases it is the same fundamental error; that is, an exaggerated use of deductive reasoning; and in all it is attended with the same result; that the higher studies are in constant danger of being disorganised by the indiscriminate application of the lower. All scientific specialists at the present time are more or less materialists, according as the phenomena they study are more or less simple and general. Geometricians, therefore, are more liable to the error than any others; they all aim consciously or otherwise at a synthesis in which the most elementary studies, those of Number, Space, and Motion, are made to regulate all the rest. But the biologists who resist this encroachment most energetically are often guilty of the same mistake. They not unfrequently attempt, for instance, to explain all sociological facts by the influence of climate and race, which are purely secondary; thus showing their ignorance of the fundamental laws of Sociology, which can only be discovered by a series of direct inductions from history.

This philosophical estimate of Materialism explains how it is that it has been brought as a charge against Positivism, and at the same time proves the deep injustice of the charge. Positivism, far from countenancing so dangerous an error, is, as we have seen, the only philosophy which can completely remove it. The error arises from certain tendencies which are in themselves legitimate, but which have been carried too far; and Positivism satisfies these tendencies in their due measure. Hitherto the evil has remained unchecked, except by the theologico-metaphysical spirit, which, by giving rise to what is called Spiritualism, has rendered a very valuable service. But useful as it has been, it could not arrest the active growth of Materialism, which has assumed in the eyes of modern thinkers something of a progressive character, from having been so long connected with the cause of resistance to a retrograde system. Notwithstanding all the protests of the spiritualists, the lower sciences have encroached upon the higher to an extent that seriously impairs their independence and their value. But Positivism meets the difficulty far more effectually. It satisfies and reconciles all that is really tenable in the rival claims of both Materialism and Spiritualism; and, having done this, it discards them both. It holds the one to be as dangerous to Order as the other to Progress. This result is an immediate consequence of the establishment of the encyclopædic scale, in which each science retains its own proper sphere of induction, while deductively it remains subordinate to the science which precedes it. But what really decides the matter is the paramount importance, both logically and scientifically, given by Positive Philosophy to social questions. For these being the questions in which the influence of Materialism is most mischievous, and also in which it is most easily introduced, a system which gives them the precedence over all others necessarily considers Materialism as obstructive as Spiritualism, both alike retarding the growth of that science for the sake of which all other sciences are studied. Further advance in the work of social regeneration implies the elimination of both of them, because it cannot proceed without exact knowledge of the laws of moral and social phenomena. . . .

With the view of securing a dispassionate consideration of this subject, and of avoiding all confusion, I have laid no stress upon the charge of immorality that is so often brought against Materialism. This reproach, even when made sincerely, is constantly belied by experience. Indeed it is inconsistent with all that we know of human nature. Our opinions, whether right or wrong, have not, fortunately, the absolute power over our feelings and conduct which is commonly attributed to them. Materialism has been provisionally connected with the whole movement of emancipation, and it has therefore often been found in common with the noblest aspirations. That connection, however, has now ceased; and it must be owned that even in the most favourable cases this error, purely intellectual though it be, has to a certain extent always checked the free play of our nobler instincts, by leading men to ignore or misconceive moral phenomena, which were left unexplained by its crude hypothesis. Cabanis, a philosopher whose moral nature was as pure and sympathetic as his intellect was elevated and enlarged, gave a striking example of this tendency in his unfortunate attack upon mediæval chivalry. The Materialism of his day had entirely blinded him to the beneficial results of the attempts made by the most energetic of our ancestors to institute the Worship of Woman.

We have now examined the two principal charges brought against the Positive system, and we have found that they apply merely to the unsystematic state in which Positive principles are first introduced. But the system is also accused of Fatalism and of Optimism; charges on which it will not be necessary to dwell at great length, because, though frequently made, they are much easier to refute.

The charge of Fatalism has accompanied every fresh extension of Positive science, from its first beginnings. Nor is this surprising; for when any series of phenomena passes from the dominion of Wills, whether modified by metaphysical abstractions or not, to the dominion of Laws, the regularity of the latter contrasts so strongly with the instability of the former, as to present an appearance of fatality, which nothing but a very careful examination of the real character of scientific truth can dissipate. And the error is the more likely to occur from the fact that our first types of natural laws are derived from the phenomena of the heavenly bodies. These, being wholly beyond our interference, always suggest the notion of absolute necessity, a notion which it is difficult to prevent from extending to more complex phenomena, as soon as they are brought within the reach of the Positive method. And it is quite true that Positivism holds the Order of Nature to be in its primary aspects strictly invariable. All variations, whether spontaneous or artificial, are only transient and of secondary import. The conception of unlimited variations would in fact be equivalent to the rejection of Law altogether. But while this accounts for the fact that every new Positive theory is accused of Fatalism, it is equally clear that blind persistence in the accusation shows a very shallow conception of what Positivism really is. For unchangeable as the Order of Nature is in its main aspects, yet all phenomena, except those of Astronomy, admit of being modified in their secondary relations, and this the more as they are more complicated. The Positive spirit, when confined to the subjects of Mathematics and Astronomy, was inevitably fatalist; but this ceased to be the case when it extended to Physics and Chemistry, and especially to Biology, where the margin of variation is very considerable. Now that it embraces Social phenomena, the reproach, however it may have been once deserved, should be heard no longer, since these phenomena, which will for the future form its principal field, admit of larger modification than any others, and that chiefly by our own intervention. It is obvious then that

Positivism, far from encouraging indolence, stimulates us to action, especially to social action, far more energetically than any Theological doctrine. It removes all groundless scruples, and prevents us from having recourse to chimeras. It encourages our efforts everywhere, except where they are manifestly useless.

For the charge of Optimism there is even less ground than for that of Fatalism. The latter was, to a certain extent, connected with the rise of the Positive spirit; but Optimism is simply a result of Theology, and its influence has always been decreasing with the growth of Positivism. Astronomical laws, it is true, suggest the idea of perfection as naturally as that of necessity. On the other hand, their great simplicity places the defects of the Order of Nature in so clear a light, that optimists would never have sought their arguments in Astronomy, were it not that the first elements of the science had to be worked out under the influence of Monotheism, a system which involved the hypothesis of absolute wisdom. But by the theory of development on which the Positive synthesis is here made to rest, Optimism is discarded as well as Fatalism, in the direct proportion of the intricacy of the phenomena. It is in the most intricate that the defects of Nature, as well as the power of modifying them, become most manifest. With regard, therefore, to social phenomena, the most complex of all, both charges are utterly misplaced. Any optimistic tendencies that writers on social subjects may display must be due to the fact that their education has not been such as to teach them the nature and conditions of the true scientific spirit. For want of sound logical training, a property peculiar to social phenomena, namely, that they exhibit a greater amount of spontaneous wisdom than might have been expected from their complexity, has been misrepresented by modern writers as though this wisdom were perfect. The phenomena in question are those of intelligent beings who are always occupied in amending the defects of their economy. It is obvious, therefore, that they will show less imperfection than if, in a case equally complicated, the agents could have been blind. The standard by which to judge of action is always to be taken relatively to the social state in which the action takes place. Therefore all historical positions and changes must have at least some grounds of justification; otherwise they would be totally incomprehensible, because inconsistent with the nature of the agents and of the actions performed by them. Now this naturally fosters a dangerous tendency to Optimism in all thinkers, who, whatever their powers may be, have not passed through any strict scientific training, and have consequently never cast off metaphysical and theological modes of thought in the higher subjects. Because every government shows a certain adaptation to the civilisation of its time, they make the loose assertion that the adaptation is perfect; a conception which is of course chimerical. But it is unjust to charge Positivism with errors which are evidently contrary to its true spirit, and merely due to the want of logical and scientific training in those who have hitherto engaged in the study of social questions. The object of Sociology is to explain all historical facts; not to justify them indiscriminately, as is done by those who are unable to distinguish the influence of the agent from that of surrounding circumstances. . . .

As the chief characteristic of Positive Philosophy is the preponderance of the social point of view through the whole range of speculation, its efficiency for the purposes of practical life is involved in the very spirit of the system. When this spirit is rightly understood, we find that it leads at once to an object far higher than that of satisfying our scientific curiosity; the object, namely, of organising human life. Conversely, this practical aspect of Positive Philosophy exercises the most salutary influence upon its speculative character. By keeping constantly before us the necessity of concentrating all scientific efforts upon the social object which constitutes their value, we take the best possible means of checking the tendency inherent in all abstract enquiries to degenerate into useless digressions. But this general connection between theory and practice would not by itself be sufficient for our purpose. It would be impossible to secure the acceptance of a mental discipline, so new and so difficult, were it not for considerations derived from the general conditions of modern society; considerations calculated to impress philosophers with a more definite sense of obligation to do their utmost towards satisfying the wants of the time. By thus arousing public sympathies and showing that the success of Positivism is a matter of permanent and general importance, the coherence of the system as well as the elevation of its aims will be placed beyond dispute. We have hitherto been regarding Positivism as the issue in which intellectual development necessarily results. We have now to view it from the social side; for until we have done this, it is impossible to form a true conception of it.

2. Dependence of Science Upon Society

. . . Scientific conviction binds men together by the mere fact of controlling their actions. The problem of reconciling men together is not in reality more difficult than that of harmonising the successive phases of each individual. The fixity of principle which results from the sense of dependence on an External Order necessarily leads to community of opinion, by at once engaging all minds in similar subjects of thought. Moreover, a common object of exertion is held up to all, that of moulding ourselves to this universal Fatality, or of modifying it. But beyond the convergence of thought and of action, which the conception of this Order produces, it has a still more direct action upon the Heart. It assists the social sympathies in their struggle against the personal propensities. It is this more sacred and less apparent influence that we are now to consider.

Its principal effect upon the character is that it disciplines Pride; an instinct which, from the impossibility of satisfying it, divides men even more than self-interest. The habit of submission is the first condition of order in human affairs. For this habit the sense of an irresistible Fatality offers the only adequate training. And it is the more effectual that it influences not merely our energies but our intellect, which is far less amenable to control. The most self-complacent metaphysician has always admitted the necessity of subordinating his reason to mathematical and astronomical truths, even whilst denying the existence of any invariable law in moral phenomena. As soon as the development of Positive thought has proceeded far enough to bring this involuntary submission into due prominence, it creates a spirit of true humility, and thus becomes consciously to ourselves a most valuable agent of moral discipline. Our reason, naturally so proud, will then have no higher aim than to become a faithful mirror of the world without us, so as to dispense by its own internal workings with the necessity for external observation; for this is what is done by scientific prevision, a power which deserves our highest admiration. This combination of submission with power is one of our noblest achievements, and

SOURCE: *Positive Polity*, Vol. I, pp. 338–43.

is at the same time a most effective agent in our moral training. Aided by the instinct of vanity, it has sometimes saved scientific men of the most servile character from a course of degradation which shocked nothing but their intelligence.

Further, the fatalities of the world and of human nature help to bring men together by reminding them that all are involved in the same miseries, and therefore stand alike in need of mutual help. Our common liability to the worst evils of life will always tend to mitigate the bitterness aroused by social inequalities, which, indeed, are themselves but a part of the same destiny. But it unites us still more strongly by the fact that being in part modifiable, it supplies a constant object for our collective or individual exertion. Thus universal Love stands out at once as the best resource for lightening the evils of life, even before men arrive at a clear consciousness that of itself it is the purest and most direct source of happiness.

Brief as the foregoing explanation has been, it will suffice as a preliminary view of a subject so intimately connected with the whole subject-matter of this Treatise. It has been shown that Science, properly so-called, whether organic or inorganic, besides being indispensable as the systematic foundation of Sociology, has of itself a deep religious value as a source of union and a means of control. The irreligious tendencies which it has hitherto called forth, and which were necessary for the first acquisition of mental freedom, are alien to the true nature of Science, the main object of which is to bind together, by demonstrating analogy or sequence. Science will always remain essential as an introduction to the final religion; and its place in the Sociocracy of the Future will be more honourable and permanent than that which incidentally was accorded to it in the ancient theocracies.

It is the consideration of this high mission which alone enables us to form a rational systematisation of the preliminary sciences. They precede and prepare the way for Sociology: but Sociology alone can co-ordinate them. The deplorable manner in which they are at present studied, shows but too clearly the need of some controlling power adequate to replace the discipline once exercised by theologico-metaphysical doctrine. For want of such a guiding principle, our scientific men have become incapable, even when sincerely desirous to do so, of explaining or of understanding the theories of their own science; having no general conceptions by which to colligate them.

Biology, for instance, looked at as an isolated system, admits of no rational or definite treatment. Starting from the incontestable principle of the general consensus of the organism, it proposes to examine the physical functions of man irrespectively of the moral functions, which can only be studied in the collective development of Humanity. This separation is permissible only on the understanding that they are afterwards studied in combination. It is merely preliminary to the normal state of the understanding, in which all Positive studies are viewed as an inseparable whole.

Inorganic Science might seem to admit of being co-ordinated into a special system irrespective of Sociology; since the phenomena which it investigates may be treated without reference to man, except as their spectator. But apart from the blame which on social grounds will attach henceforth to this Utopia of mathematicians, its value intellectually is of the most superficial kind. For the domain of research, being unbounded, would, if independently treated, encourage unlimited digressions, such as not only would be utterly barren, but would render all systematisation hopeless. Objective unity in this field is impossible, as the fruitless endeavours of the last two centuries have shown. It admits by its very nature of none but subjective unity: that is to say, of unity produced by the predominance of the human or social point of view. This is the only universal connection between the doctrines, and even between the methods of physical science; and by means of it the treatment of each subject, however exhaustless, can be restricted to what is really required for the sacred purpose of devoting all our efforts to the continuous service of Humanity.

But the restriction of the preliminary sciences here laid down, and which is involved in considering them merely as a necessary introduction to the final science, is of even greater importance to Feeling than it is to Reason and to the Active faculties. The charge of immorality so often brought in modern times against scientific study, illogically as it may be expressed, contains, and always will contain, an element of truth.

I have already spoken . . . of the materialistic tendencies necessarily involved in the pursuit of the lower sciences when uncontrolled by the authority of the higher. Following this thought still further we shall find that all intellectual culture, however systematic, has a tendency to vitiate character, not only by inducing hardness of feeling, but by developing pride. The great personal efforts which it requires arouse an exaggerated sense of individuality, which effaces and perverts our conception of the universal connection of the whole human race: a connection as unquestionable in this aspect as in every other. Everywhere it is the Great Being who in reality produces, although its organs must always be individual. In practical life we are far less apt to forget this connection; constant co-operation being here of immediate necessity. In this department metaphysical self-sufficiency has never ventured upon its absurd fiction of universal construction by the unaided efforts of an individual. But intellectual life is always liable to these mischievous and anti-social illusions of pride; and it can only be preserved from them by the constant control of religion, guiding it ever back to its high purpose.

Difficult as the introduction of such principles in the present day may seem, it is assuredly not impracticable. We must not carry our censure of modern intellect so far as to imagine it permanently disqualified from accepting the just supremacy of the heart. Its state of insurrection has been for a long time justified by the inevitable necessity of breaking through a most oppressive bondage. Morally that insurrection has been disastrous; yet in the nobler types of scientific eminence it has always evoked an obscure consciousness of the social and philosophic construction which would be the ultimate justification of their partial and preparatory efforts. A clear proof that the modern spirit is really tending in the direction of wise religious discipline is the way in which the final religion has arisen. For, as I showed clearly in my System of Positive Philosophy, Positivism originated in intellectual considerations, although now it has established direct and continuous relations with Feeling. Strong therefore as is the pride of science, it has yet yielded to the urgency of social considerations, and permitted the Intellect to rise above its condition of utter anarchy, and voluntarily to restore the Heart to its normal position of preponderance. The only discipline to which modern thought is radically opposed is that of retrograde principles. It invites such discipline as will ennoble its position and secure its progress by concentrating it upon high moral and political problems, from which, for want of sound principles, it has hitherto been debarred. As for those minds of an inferior stamp who cling to anarchy because it favours their self-importance, the new religion will soon counteract and suppress their influence, hostile as it is to the best interests of society. Such minds are reduced in the present position of affairs to one of two alternatives; either they must concede the principle of the preponderance of the Heart over the Intellect; or they must confess that the systematic demonstration of that principle is too difficult for them to follow. . . .

Whether we look then at the more systematic requirements of the Future, or at the empirical necessities of the past, we are alike led to the conclusion that the preparatory sciences, organic or inorganic, are to be viewed as directly or indirectly introductory to the one final science of Humanity. These preliminary studies have in themselves, moreover, a high religious value; as serving to regulate and to maintain the existence of the Supreme Being. It is in one or other of these two aspects that they are henceforth to be regarded, with the exception of course of their various applications to the corresponding arts. Submission to such salutary discipline and consecration to so high a purpose cannot fail to imbue them with sympathetic feeling; in such a way that the austerest meditations may be transformed into acts of love. Love, and action under the influence of love, will be the dominant feature of human life in the small minority of true philosophers, as in every other class. It is their especial privilege that not action merely, but thought is regulated by love; because the nature of their high calling brings them into direct contact with the highest functions of the Great Being. It might seem that thought would be restricted by such discipline as this; its real purpose is to enlarge the principal field of thought by preserving it from the useless digressions to which it is so prone. These often culpable abuses of the scientific spirit, taking the means for the end, will be strictly repressed on grounds of public and even of personal morality, as wasting for purposes of puerile vanity forces which it is of the greatest importance to economise. And there will be the less scruple in the exercise of this wholesome control, that popular instinct, when guided by religion, will feel that underneath this pretended zeal for the discovery of truth lies a real impotence to deal with the more important problems, these being also the more difficult. True, there was once a logical utility in speculations which had no scientific value; but this was only in the period of preparatory development. Now that the Positive method is thoroughly instituted in all its parts, and that the general purpose for which Science exists has been clearly manifested, there is no longer any excuse for mere academical specialities, and Western Europe will soon cease to afford them any systematic encouragement.

3. Intellectual Progress Can Ultimately Be Appreciated Through the Development of Humanity

. . . We can never suppose that the faculty from which we derive all our knowledge of laws, either within or without us, was ever regarded as having no laws of its own. The traces of the laws in our mental constitution are found in the least of our discoveries, physical or moral; since but for laws of mind, none would be possible. But the scientific understanding of this mental constitution offers more difficulties than either that of the material world, or of our moral nature; because it rests in reality upon the gradual progress of the entire race. The life of the individual gives us enough means of perceiving the main Moral laws by themselves; although they appear at first sight devoid of any connection. On the contrary, the progress of the intellect is not perceptible in individual life in so marked a manner as to enable the leading Intellectual laws to be directly studied in individuals. These can only be seen unmistakably in the entire series of the phases through which the mind of Humanity has passed. This important discovery requires therefore that Positive Doctrine should be extended to the social sphere; and in so doing it is led to form itself completely, and necessarily takes in the moral laws. Thus the establishment of the laws of mind must nearly coincide with that of true Religion.

The principal difficulty, therefore, in the formation of the Positive Doctrine consists in the regular succession of several great phases of thought or sciences; each of which depends on the preceding, and yet they only produce a religious influence when combined in one whole. Each of these successive sciences requires its own special inductions; but they cannot be reduced to a system except by the deductive method called out by all the less complex sciences. Were it not for this natural series, conforming to the mode in which phenomena depend on each other, the laws of nature would be not less incoherent than irrational. When ranged in this classification, the sciences lowest in the scale communicate to those above

SOURCE: *Positive Polity*, Vol. II, pp. 32-33.

them that character of regularity and fixity, which is due to their simplicity, whilst they receive down from those above them the dignity, which belongs to those of a higher rank. The religious influence of a Philosophy of Reality arises from this action and reaction between the different elements that compose it. These are the conditions indispensable to a true conviction of the fundamental fixity of the order of the universe. The best type of it is found in the celestial phenomena, for they alone are removed from any interference from man.

4. The Synthesis of Science Is Dependent Upon
Positivist Humanitarianism

Subject to the inevitable control of moral science, all scientific theories cleared of misdirected investigations take a sacred and synthetical character, as being definitive portions of the body of Positive doctrine, which, step by step, in the natural course of things, has been formed by their contributions. Science, thus renovated, regains with greater completeness and stability the majestic unity it attained under the fostering care of the Theocracy. . . . The speciality without unity, which has hitherto been the great feature of modern scientific enquiry, reduces it in truth wellnigh to the level of empiricism, with an exception for Mathematics. And even in Mathematics, the scientific character is but too often purely superficial, since the prevalence of the tendency to substitute the combination of signs for the higher processes of thought, or at any rate, to make the latter subordinate. All the other branches of natural philosophy are so completely given over to anarchy and consequent retrogression, that religion alone, with its power of direction and repression, can introduce discipline and prevent the dissolution of the whole system. Now, for a state of synthesis, it is imperative that every Positive theory, normally viewed, become an affluent of the science by which man studies his nature in order to guide his conduct. For we are still under the dominion of analysis so long as the laws of the inorganic world, with their complement, the laws of life, are not referred directly to the laws of man's social

SOURCE: *Positive Polity*, Vol. IV, pp. 48–49.

and individual existence—the domain of Humanity, the sole fountain of intellectual unity.

5. All Phenomena Are Human*

. . . Strictly speaking, there is no phenomenon within our cognisance which is not in the truest sense human, and that not merely because it is man who takes cognisance of it, but also from the purely objective point of view, man summarising in himself all the laws of the world, as the ancients rightly felt. Yet each class of attributes must be studied with reference to the simplest cases; that is, in beings where it exists, if not isolated, at any rate freed from all complication with the higher attributes, which we eliminate provisionally by abstraction, the better to understand their foundations. Thus beginning with the simplest phenomena, we gradually increase the complication of our enquiries by the introduction in succession of higher properties, so training ourselves by a course of decreasing abstraction for the normal state of the scientific reason. When we have reached it, we enter on the regime of complete synthesis, the regime in which man, viewed directly as indivisible by nature, is the constant object of all theories calculated to make him more fit for the service of the Great Being. Abstraction thus loses its scientific preeminence and retains solely its logical utility; we habitually concentrate all our efforts on the most important problems, recurring to the lower only to meet the wants, in particular respects, of the higher domain.

6. Sociology as the Universal Point of View†

The only really universal point of view is the human, or, speaking more exactly, the social. This is the only one which recurs and is perpetually renewed, in every department of thought; in regard to the external world as well as to Man. Thus, if we want to conceive of the rights of the sociological spirit to supremacy, we have only

* SOURCE: *Positive Polity*, Vol. IV, p. 161.
† SOURCE: *Positive Philosophy*, pp. 793–94.

to regard all our conceptions . . . as so many necessary results of a series of determinate phases, proper to our mental evolution, personal and collective, taking place according to invariable laws, statical and dynamical, which rational observation is competent to disclose. Since philosophers have begun to meditate deeply on the intellectual phenomena, they have always been more or less convinced, in spite of all prepossession, of the inevitable reality of these fundamental laws; for their existence is always supposed in every study, in which any conclusion whatever would be impossible if the formation and variation of our opinions were not subject to a regular order, independent of our will, and the pathological change of which is known to be in no way arbitrary. But, besides the extreme difficulty of the subject, and its vicious management hitherto, human reason being capable of growth only in social circumstances, it is clear that no decisive discovery could be made in this way till society should have attained a generality of view which was not possible till our day. Imperfect as sociological study may yet be, it furnishes us with a principle which justifies and guides its intervention, scientific and logical, in all the essential parts of the speculative system, which can thus alone be brought into unity. It appears to me that the mere existence of this book is a sufficient testimony to the reality and fertility of the new general philosophy; for it presents the spectacle of the whole range of sciences subjected to one point of view, without interference with the independence of any, and with a confirmation instead of a weakening of their respective characters, by the power of a single thought—by the application of a single general law. . . . Thoughtful readers can not but be aware of the new light, generated by the creation of Sociology, cast upon all the foregoing sciences. Considering the inorganic sciences alone, in which such philosophical intervention is most questioned, we shall find the following results:

1. In Chemistry, the conception of facultative dualism, by which difficulties in high chemical speculation may be dealt with which had hitherto appeared insurmountable:

2. In Physics, the foundation of a sound theory of scientific hypotheses, for want of which the positivity of the leading conception was seriously impaired:

3. In Astronomy, the just estimate of sidereal astronomy, and the reduction of our researches to our own system:

4. In Mathematics, the rectification of the basis of Rational Me

chanics, of the whole system of geometrical conceptions, and of the first procedures of analysis, ordinary and transcendental.

All these improvements, tending alike to consolidation and advancement, are due, more or less directly, to the supremacy of the historical view proper to sociology; the only view which permits our first and constant attention to be given to the statical and dynamical working out of questions relating to the respective constitution of the various parts of natural philosophy.

We may thus fairly decide that the philosophical principle of unity is afforded by Sociology, and not by Mathematics. As the varying constitution of the speculative class necessarily represents the corresponding situation of the human mind in general, the nascent positivism of the last three centuries has given to the mathematicians more and more of that authority which, till the end of the mediæval period, had belonged to moral and social researches. This provisional anomaly will now come to an end; for, when sociological theory has once reached the positive state, there is nothing except the opposition of the ignorant and the interested to prevent the human view from resuming its natural place at the head of all human speculation. I have said that this conclusion was not only the first but the greatest: and in fact, the question of supremacy is the only one important to decide. . . . The only possible alternative is now decided, by considerations drawn from abstract science alone, according to the original conditions of this Work;—that abstract science which, after Bacon, I have called the First Philosophy, because it is the basis of all speculation whatever; but the same decision may be reached by considerations of concrete science, and even by æsthetic contemplation: for the sociological organization of positive philosophy favors their expansion; whereas the mathematical mode, if fully carried out, would be fatal to it.

7. Positivist Sociology and Public Opinion

. . . All views of the future condition of society, the views of practical men as well as of philosophic thinkers, agree in the belief that the principal feature of the state to which we are tending will

SOURCE: *Positive Polity*, Vol. I, pp. 110–14.

be the increased influence which Public Opinion is destined to exercise.

It is in this beneficial influence that we shall find the surest guarantee for morality; for domestic and even for personal morality, as well as for social. For as the whole tendency of Positivism is to induce everyone to live as far as possible without concealment, the public will be intrusted with a strong check upon the life of the individual. Now that all theological illusions have become so entirely obsolete, the need of such a check is greater than it was before. It compensates for the insufficiency of natural goodness which we find in most men, however wisely their education has been conducted. Except the noblest of joys, that which springs from social sympathy when called into constant exercise, there is no reward for doing right so satisfactory as the approval of our fellow beings. Even under theological systems it has been one of our strongest aspirations to live esteemed in the memory of others. And still more prominence will be given to this noble form of ambition under Positivism, because it is the only way now left of satisfying the inward desire of prolonging life beyond the present. And the increased force of Public Opinion will correspond to the increased necessity for it. The peculiar reality of Positive doctrine and its constant conformity with facts facilitate the recognition of its principles, and remove all obscurity in their application. They are not to be evaded by subterfuges like those to which metaphysical and theological principles, from their vague and absolute character have been always liable. Again, the primary principle of Positivism which is to judge every question by the standard of social interests is in itself a direct appeal to Public Opinion; since the public is naturally the judge of the good or bad effect of action upon the common welfare. Under theological and metaphysical systems no appeal of this sort was recognised; because the objects upheld as the highest aims of life were purely personal.

14

Miscellany

1. Sociology and Education

With the advent of positivism, education must become positivist. That is, recognition of the underlying unity of all science is essential to education, along with the ultimate understanding that benevolence and love are the final aim and object of a life guided by positivism. Reason is fostered so that emotion can lead to intelligent action and cement social solidarity. Comte is an early proponent of free public secularized education and an opponent of a formal schooling restricted to aristocrats and the wealthy.

Comte had little use for the educational system in vogue in his day. It was not based on the sciences, beginning with mathematics and culminating in sociology—thus the individual mind could not develop into a universal mind as a student lived through the stages of mental development himself and saw their interconnection. For Comte, the positivist education of workingmen was a debt owed to them by the Republic and through the educated workingmen the Republic would flourish.

With that unusual foresight he so often manifests, Comte sees the importance of the family (particularly the mother) in initiating the education of the child. To be sure, no one in Comte's time fully understood, in psychological terms, how the family may also have a negative effect on talents.

Comte did not expect much from the formal academies of France in behalf of the workingman. The academies were tied to a theological or metaphysical past whereas positivism was indissolubly linked to a secular future. He did not, however, expect every worker to be a scientist but rather held that the moral disposition inherent in positivism would be developed in the worker through appropriate education.

Great books were to be the basis of education. Comte foresaw that the positivist "priesthood" could recruit individuals from the general public who would become philosophers themselves. Finally, he even hoped that the staid institutions of learning would take over positivist education and transform themselves through reorganization along positivist lines so that even the most learned in the old sense would come to be dedicated to the ideal of humanitarianism.

Material on Comte's sociology of education is found in Positive Philosophy, pp. 492–97; Positive Polity, Vol. I, pp. 138–47, and Vol. IV, pp. 236–39.

2. Sociology of Art

To those nurtured on neo-positivism (that is, the distortion of Comte's doctrine along so-called physicalistic lines) his heavy emphasis on the necessity for art in a positivist society may come as something of a shock. But this shock occurs because of the long-standing failure to come to grips with Comte's view of the primacy of "feeling" over "reason." The search for appropriate ideals by which men may live is in no small part met by artists' revamping of current values. Art has been looked upon as a heritage of the past rather than as a harbinger of the future. But indeed, Comte writes: "The greatest epoch of Art has yet to come."

Scientific genius and artistic genius are two sides of the same coin— the state of society. To be sure, some periods of the philosophical regeneration of science have preceded great advances in art so that a renaissance in art may depend upon philosophical reorientation. But science and art are not "two cultures" as one contemporary view would have it; they become dual only when their philosophical unity is undermined or misunderstood.

Yet, great positivist art must await the further development of positivist society which it will mirror. The proper study of man is through positivism; the glorification of man will be the aim of positivist art.

Comte does not disparage earlier poets, architects, sculptors, musicians, and painters but he does see the limitations set upon their work by the state of society in which they appear. The past and the present may show us this unilateral restriction. But the future of high art will be furthered by positivism, not limited by it. The past can provide no more than models and relationships. This view can become retrograde as in the aggrandizement of antiquity, or negative as in the emancipation of the artist through the modern revolution without art itself becoming populist. Art under positivism will concern itself with all men and not pander as in the past to the few who hold power or control wealth. Such art will enhance human action by arousing in the proletariat that benevolence which is basic to positivist society. The study of art will become part of universal education and help to make men cosmopolitan and international in outlook. What was formerly mere adornment for the workers will become their right as the backbone of positivist society.

Students of the sociology of art will find highly enlightening Comte's discussion in Positive Philosophy, pp. 706–16, and in Positive Polity, Vol. I, pp. 220–22, 227–34, 240–42, 246–47, 249–56.

3. The Emancipation of Women

Seen from the vantage point of the present day, Comte's views on women sound puerile. But within the context of the historical period in which he wrote, cloying as his ideas on women sound today, his views mark a decided step forward. His attitude is in line with John Stuart Mill's attack on the subjugation of women, with the rise of the suffragette and woman's rights movements, and with women's final triumph in becoming full-fledged citizens.

Though tangential to his discussion of women under what he called Sociolatry (the worship of society), attention must be called to Comte's clearheadedness as expressed at the end of the chapter on women in volume one of Positive Polity as follows:

And with all the agencies, physical or moral, which can be brought to bear, we shall have to acknowledge that the exceeding imperfection of human nature interposes permanent obstacles to the object for which Positivism strives, the victory of social sympathy over self-love.

A few short excerpts from Positive Polity will serve to give some indication of Comte's views on women and their importance in a positivist society.

The organisation of moral force is based on the alliance of philosophers with the people; but the adhesion of women is necessary to its completion. The union of all three initiates the movement of social regeneration which is to bring the revolution to a close. But more than this: their union is at once an inauguration of the final order of society. Each of these three elements will be acting as it will be called upon to act in the normal state, and will be occupying its permanent position relatively to the temporal power. The philosophic class whose work it is to combine the action of the other two classes will find valuable assistance from women in every family, as well as powerful co-operation from the people in every city. The result will be a combination of all the classes who stand apart from political administration, formed with a view of subjecting all practical measures to the fixed rules of universal morality. Exceptional cases will arise where moral influence is insufficient; in these it will be necessary for the people to interfere actively. But philosophers and women are dispensed from such interference. Direct action would be most injurious to their powers of sympathy or meditation. They can only preserve these powers by keeping clear of all positions of political authority.

But the moral force resulting from this combined action, while more efficient than that of the Middle Ages, will impose conditions of great difficulty on its systematic organs. From the Priest of Humanity high powers of intellect are required; and a heart worthy of such intellect. To secure the support of women, and the co-operation of the people, he must have the sympathy and purity of the first, the energy and disinterestedness of the second. Such natures are rare; yet without them the new spiritual power cannot obtain that ascendancy over society to which Positivism aspires. [Vol. I, pp. 218–19.]

As examples of the highest attributes of man there is no lack in the world of living personifications of the Supreme Being. Every man of feeling can recognise them in the special qualities of the tender sex; and see them as the natural prerogatives of every woman worthy of the name. When by a true system the instinctive tendency of our nature is brought to its perfection, and our artificial Order has developed the natural Order of the world, this quality in woman will enable us to meet all the difficulties which arise from the subjective nature of the Great Being. Superior in power of affection, more able to keep both the intellectual and the active powers in continual subordination to feeling, women are formed as the natural intermediaries between Humanity and men. This is their high mission in the Religion of demonstration. The Great Being confides especially to them its moral Providence; maintaining through them the direct and constant cultivation of universal affection, in the midst of all the distractions of thought or action, which are for ever withdrawing men from its influence. The uniformity in their natures and position shows still more clearly this quality in woman. Lastly, this high office is that which best sustains the objective action of the living by the subjective influence of the dead. For a true woman cannot really die in the chief of all her functions, that of forming men.

To proceed from the general to the special consideration of this subject. Beside the uniform influence of every woman on every man, to attach him to Humanity, such is the importance and the difficulty of this ministry, that each of us should be placed under the special guidance of one of these angels, to answer for him, as it were, to the Great Being. This moral guardianship may assume three types: the mother, the wife, and the daughter; each having several modifications. . . . Together, they form the three simple modes of solidarity, or unity with contemporaries—obedience, union, and protection—as well as the three degrees of continuity between the ages, by uniting us with the past, the present, and the future. In accordance with my theory of the brain each corresponds with one of our three altruistic instincts: veneration, attachment, and benevolence. This theory shows that for a complete protection all three types of angels must be constantly conjoined; and where deficient naturally, they must be supplied by types of our own choosing. The union of all three forms that first ideal in the gradually enlarging spheres, both moral and mental, through which we rise to the conception of the Great Being. [Vol. II, pp. 56–57.]

For the Western Revolution . . . [women] never felt any genuine sympathy comparable to that with which they had hailed the advent of Catholicism. But this holy resistance of the loving sex is far from deserving to be regarded as an obstruction: on the contrary, it ought to be put at the head of the organising forces of the Modern Movement, which thus was saved from a total rupture with the Middle Age, and Chivalry, its sum and substance. The problem then before Humanity could never have been finally solved had that bond with the past been lost. Women preserved it. They thus took a profound part in the Western Revolution as a whole, notwithstanding their repugnance to its subversive and dispersive tendencies, which, though necessary as a preparation for the future, starved the Heart. By such antipathy, so constant and so legitimate, Women spontaneously indicated the final condition of the Modern Transition: which could not issue in the true regeneration of society, unless the loving sex cooperated by upholding the paramount claims of the Affections; claims which are at last satisfied by Positivism. [Vol. III, p. 436.]

. . . Personal worship is characterised above all by the heartfelt adoration of the affective sex, on the ground of the inherent capacity of every true woman to be a representative of Humanity. As composite, the highest form of existence can hardly be appreciated unless personified. All its true servants are, in their several degrees, each by virtue of his leading attribute, capable of representing it. But as sympathy is the great source of unity, and sympathy is strongest in woman, woman must be the best personification of a being, the foundation of whose existence, as a whole, is love. Woman, the spontaneous embodiment of the Family idea, alone can worthily represent any collective existence; the instinct of the race made her the emblem of the Country before as yet she had gained the estimation which should qualify her for the representative of Humanity. [Vol. IV, p. 96.]

4. Concentration of Capital and Political Power

Karl Marx was disdainful of Comte and his new science of sociology. This disdain was rooted in good part both in Comte's willingness to accept private ownership of property under capitalism, including the concentration of wealth, rather than to espouse secular socialism, and in his acceptance of the rule by force rather than the eventual "withering away of the state." This latter idea of Marx's was spelled out by Lenin in The State and Revolution.

For Comte, concentration of capital is inevitable. Capitalist accumulation arises from the advance of the material life of civilization and this accumulation necessarily leads to concentration by the owners of private property. But such private ownership would be checked in its exercise of power by the spiritual power which would be based on the hierarchy of moral worth rather than of material worth. Raymond Aron has pointed out that Comte's views here have not had great effect upon economic thought except on the extreme political right and left wings.

Likewise, force as the basis of the state did not disturb Comte, whether such political force was based on numbers or on wealth. This coercive power would be offset by spiritual power which would regulate the inner life of man and control the use of temporal power. As Comte phrases his views here, they sound extremely naïve. Yet, if we re-phrase them in contemporary terms, the spiritual power becomes public law which regulates and controls abuses of concentrated wealth and eventually brings forth what we today call "the welfare state." For Comte, economics and politics in positivist society would be subservient to science and ethics. Once positivist science and the ethics of humanitarian ideals gained sway, economics and politics would fall into what he considered their proper, and secondary, place.

For a short summary of Comte's position here the reader is referred to Raymond Aron's Main Currents in Sociological Thought, Vol. I, pp. 71–3, 93, 98.

5. Toward the Religion of Humanity

Comte's reputation has suffered from serious misunderstanding of the Religion of Humanity. To be sure, the priesthood status he assigned to leaders of positivism, the rituals and ceremonials, the new calender by day, week, and month, the concept of the Great Being, and his idea of himself as the first vice-regent of the Great Being all have a megalomanic aura. But what he was aiming for was and is not foolish. It was the outline of a faith by which men might live and which would bring "reason" under the auspices of "feeling"—veneration, submission, and benevolence.

In Positive Philosophy, he had brought together the sciences by comprehending their philosophical unity through positivism and the pervasiveness of the sociological point of view. In Positive Polity, on the other hand, he tried to show that humanitarianism (the supremacy of love and sympathy in action) alone would bring philosophy into the realm of mundane human life. Instead of aristocracy and what he considered the vagaries of democracy he offered "Sociocracy." The sociocrats would be the leaders of positivist society, supremely learned but not narrowly academic, tempering the application of their learning with sympathy. True positivists would accept the principles of both the Cours and the Polity. The

Cours ennobles science and the Polity ennobles human life in general.

It is of contemporary interest that Comte points out that positivism alone can meet the challenge of Communism and will entail a more radical transformation of society than that envisaged by Communism. As we saw in the last section, positivism would control the power of the wealthy and check the abuse of political power by leaders of government.

Comte sees positivism with its culmination in the Religion of Humanity as a mass movement in process of development. He did not expect it to take hold instantaneously but to gather adherents over time. What has actually happened, since Comte's time, is that positivism as a faith and a movement has declined and has been assimilated into the international movement known as Humanism. Meanwhile, it altered the course of the philosophy of science and started sociology off on its long course of development. Perhaps when sociology as a discipline has met the challenge thrown out by Comte, we shall be more in readiness for the empathy which will lead toward the peace and security that he wished for mankind.

His views on this subject may be found in Positive Polity, Vol. IV, pp. 455–71. An example of how the Religion of Humanity would operate in a positivist society under the aegis of the Supreme Being already appeared in this book in Chapter XIV, section 3, which deals with Comte's views on women.